Scattered To The Four Winds

An Acadian Family's Journey

R M Lucie Comeau-Kroshus

Copyright © 2023 RM Lucie Comeau-Kroshus
All rights reserved.

All rights reserved in all media. No part of this book may be used, reproduced, stored in a retrieval system or transmitted in any form or by any means without prior written permission of the author.

This is a work of fiction. However, all of the characters are real, all of the places are real and all of the events happened to the best of the author's research. The conversations and dialogues were created by the author's imagination. On occasion, certain, very small, liberties were taken with chronology. The author has put forth her best efforts to tell a truthful story.

Book design, cover and artwork by: Lucie Comeau-Kroshus

ISBN (print): 978-1-7388119-0-8
ISBN (hardcover): 978-1-7388119-2-2
ISBN (ebook): 978-1-7388119-1-5

First Edition: May 2023

Published by:
RM Lucie Comeau-Kroshus, Moose Jaw, Saskatchewan, Canada
luciecomeaukroshus@hotmail.com

For my father,
who possessed
all of the gentle
traits of his
Acadian forefathers –
he was loving,
patient, kind,
peaceful, proud,
loyal, hardworking,
and independent in spirit.

Author's Forward

Scattered to the Four Winds was written for two reasons. The first is to record as accurately as possible the history of our family's journey from Acadia to Quebec to Minnesota to Saskatchewan.

The second reason was to shine a light on the Acadian people. When I began reading about our ancestors, I was immediately enamoured. The stories unanimously portrayed the Acadians as loving, caring, joyful and peaceful; a group content to live a bucolic lifestyle, apathetic about material possessions and wealth. This reminded me of one person: my father.

My father, Harry Comeau Jr. was born in Saskatchewan in 1930, three months after his father had passed away. He was a man who was never mean, overbearing, belittling, jealous, or angry. He was never boastful, loud, obnoxious, or demanding. He never spoke poorly of another individual. My father was always kind, loving, patient, and inclusive. He treated everyone equally, with respect and dignity, regardless of their circumstances. His glass was never half empty; it was always full and overflowing!

The Acadians believed in living life with a pure heart and this aligned perfectly with my father's convictions. My father lived every day of his life in accordance with those beliefs. This story is written in his voice, in his memory and in his honour.

RM Lucie Comeau-Kroshus

Family Tree

Pierre Comeau & Rose Bayon
- Etienne Comeau & Marie Anne Lefebvre
- Pierre the eldest Comeau & Jeanne Bourg
- Marie Francoise Comeau & Jean Gaudet
- Jean the eldest Comeau & Francoise Hebert / Catherine Joseph
- Pierre the youngest & Jeanne Bourgeois
- Antoine Comeau & Wooden Dorcus
- Jeanne Comeau & Etienne Hebert
- Marie Anne Comeau & Etienne Rivet
- Jean the youngest & Catherine Babin

Pierre the eldest Comeau & Jeanne Bourg

- Marie Anne Comeau & Claude Pitre
- Abraham Comeau & Marie Marguerite Pitre
- Marguerite Comeau & Maurice Vigneau
- Anne Comeau & Francois Raymond
- Marie Jeanne Comeau & Pierre Thibeau
- Joseph Comeau & Marie Roy
- Pierre Comeau
- Marie Madeleine Comeau & Francois Langlois
- Angelique Comeau & Jacques Lord
- Elisabeth Comeau & Claude Thibodeau
- Catherine Comeau
- Francoise Comeau & Charles Thibodeau
- Cecile Comeau
- Jean Comeau & Magdeleine Amireau
- Francois Comeau & Anne Lord
- Maurice Comeau & Marguerite Thibodeau
- Ambroise Comeau & Marguerite Cormier
- Jacques Comeau

Francois Comeau & Anne Lord

- Marie Anne Comeau & Jean Baptiste Landry / Louis Rousse
- Maurice Comeau & Brigitte Savoie
- Marguerite Comeau
- Marie Madeleine Comeau & Joseph Michel
- Elisabeth Comeau & Jean Baptiste Michel
- Charles Comeau
- Francois Comeau & Marie Francoise Paris / Marie Genevieve Dubois
- Anastasie Comeau & Michel Rivard
- Joseph Comeau & Marguerite Vincent

Francois Comeau & Marie Francoise Paris

- Agathe Comeau & Antoine Dubois
- Elisabeth Comeau & Eloi Belanger

Francois Comeau & Marie Genevieve Dubois

- Marie Josephe Comeau & Joseph Tourigny
- Marguerite Comeau
- Angelique Comeau & Joseph Picher
- Marie Anne Comeau
- Marguerite Comeau & Antoine Deshayes
- Francois Comeau & Marie Beauchesne
- Marie Genevieve Comeau & Joseph Lacourse
- Charles Comeau & Genevieve Beaudet
- Marie Anne Comeau
- Michel Jerome Comeau & Marie Angele Parmentier

Michel Jerome Comeau & Marie Angele Parmentier

- Olivier Comeau
- Elzear Comeau & Celina Doucet / Francoise Leblanc
- Alexis Comeau &Madeleine Deshaies
- Noel Comeau & Marie Alice Provencher
- Reine Comeau
- Aurelie Comeau & Jean Goupil
- Felix Comeau & Henriette Doucet

Elzear Comeau & Celina Doucet

- Agnes Comeau & Luc Piche
- Melanie Comeau & Joseph Bourque
- Virginie Comeau & Julien Richards
- Marie Ursule Comeau
- Leah Comeau & Victor Cormier
- Pierre Joseph Comeau
- Phileas Comeau & Marie Cormier
- Onesiphore Comeau & Leonie Bellefueille
- Omer Comeau & Melanie Heon
- Marie Celinie Comeau

Elzear Comeau & Francoise Leblanc

- Joseph Albert Comeau & Marie Bergeron
- Joseph Arsene Comeau
- Joseph Arthur Comeau & Delphine Bergeron
- Marie Rosana Comeau

Arthur Comeau & Delphine Bergeron/Arthur St. Hilaire

- Harry Comeau Sr. & Emilie Guigon
- Norman Comeau & Olivia Bertrand
- Ena Comeau & Emilien Ethier
- Clarence Comeau & Anne Pozi
- Louis Comeau & Marguerite Roy

Harry Comeau Sr. & Emilie Guigon

- Andre Comeau & Laurette Dupuis
- Harry Comeau Jr. & Jeanne Blondeau

Chapter 1

Ste. Gertrude, Quebec – 1869

My great-grandfather, Elzear Comeau, was in the graveyard digging a hole. There was nothing unusual about that. It was his job. He was the church sexton for the parish of Ste. Gertrude, charged with the maintenance of its buildings and grounds. He took great pride in keeping the premises clean, overseeing the town graveyard, and digging the graves. He was responsible for the guardianship of the holy vessels, the holy books, and the parish registers. He opened the doors to the sacred edifice and summoned the faithful to hear the word of the Lord.

Elzear was well known in the parish. He had dug the graves for many of his relatives, including his mother three years prior, and his numerous friends and acquaintances. He had buried enough people to populate a small town, and he remembered them all. He treated each burial with great care, respecting the innate dignity of the human body.

It was a cold mid-November day. The snow had not started to fall yet, but most of the leaves had abandoned the trees, except for a few stubborn caramel-coloured oak ones. The ground was partly frozen but that had never stalled or hindered Elzear's work. At forty-five-years old, he was fit as a fiddle and could handle the digging work easily. He had all his tools at the ready, a shovel, a pick, and a mattock. A wooden frame template built to the prescribed specifications of the deceased, was placed on the ground over the intended grave. He was ready to dig the hole, but he struggled with the first shovelful of dirt. It was not the physical act that challenged him. It was the heart-wrenching psychological distress. In just a couple of days, he would ring the church bells to announce the funeral of his beloved wife, Celina Comeau (Doucet).

Inside the parish registry, where all the records for the baptisms, marriages, and deaths were kept, Elzear's signature appeared frequently. Since he was always on the church grounds working, he could be called upon at a moment's notice to witness an event. Of course his signature was seldom needed for the joyous occasions of weddings and baptisms when large gatherings of family members came to celebrate. For these events, witnesses were plentiful. But his signature appeared beside the many deaths recorded, primarily those of newborn children, lifeless in their parents' arms, as the priest blessed them and read the scriptures. It was always the same scripture that was read and it was always the same entry written in the registry; only the names and dates changed.

Elzear was not a large man, but he was outgoing, boisterous, and energetic. He had a large personality, and his penmanship revealed it. The name 'Elzear Comeau' was usually written in oversized looping letters resembling a primary grade student just learning his cursives. His letters lacked uniformity, graceful turns, and flourishes. His name would be sprawled across the entire registry's page, interspersed with ink blobs, indicating that he struggled with the fountain pen. In addition, the spelling was always inconsistent: Elzear with two 'r's' or Elzear ending with an 'e'; Comeau often contained two 'm's'. However, it was evident from his numerous signatures in the parish registry that he had witnessed many, many deaths.

Celina was six months shy of her twenty-first birthday, a minor, when she married Elzear in January, 1851. She was baptized Marie Dina, entry B52 in the La-Nativite-de-Notre-Dame-de-Becancour parish registry, born June 15, 1831, to Moyse Doucet, and Marie LeVasseur.

Through their eighteen years of marriage, Elzear and Celina had ten children. There were five girls in a row, Agnes, Melanie, Ursule, Leah and Virginie. Then came four boys, Pierre, Phileas, Onesifore and Omer and lastly baby, Marie.

Before Celina gave birth to her last child, she became ill. One morning she struggled to get out of bed and tend to the children and the house. Within a few months she had become thin, pale-skinned, weak, and exhausted.

The doctor had diagnosed her with tuberculosis. External fatigue, flushed cheeks, bright eyes, loss of appetite, night sweats, and a general wasting away of the victim were the most common characteristics of this disease. It was commonly referred to as the White Plague or Consumption and had been the leading cause of death in Canada for the past several years.

Without hesitation, their fourteen-year-old daughter, Ursule, took charge of the care of her mother. She continually brought her nursing cups of herbal teas, hoping to exorcise the infection from her mother's body, but Celina's symptoms worsened as each new day emerged. Elzear had watched with great pain and sadness as the condition ravaged her body and she faded away. Two months after baby Marie was born, Celina passed away leaving my great-grandfather with nine children.

On the morning of November fifteenth, three days after Celina's death, the bells from each tower at Ste. Gertrude's church began to ring. It was one of my great-grandfather's duties to ring the bells for Sunday worship, funerals and weddings. But it required two men to coordinate the efforts and ring the bells from the two towers.

"Merci Antoine," Elzear thanked his good friend Antoine Leblanc for helping him.

"You ring the first bell," Antoine replied as they climbed to the top of the towers. "I will join in at the correct time, and keep the rhythm going."

A coordinated effort was needed between the two men to make the bells toll, very slowly, one at a time, with a significant gap between the strikes. Bong! One second, two seconds, three seconds. Bong! One second, two seconds, three seconds. Bong! The technique was commonly used to signify a funeral, to make the congregation aware that a beloved one had passed away.

There were many dedicated parishioners willing to help Elzear, because they were faithful to God's house and the church meant everything to them. Each Sunday morning, come rain or shine, they would assemble to attend mass. They all knew that it was a mortal sin not to attend mass, and a mortal sin, they believed, was like a one-way ticket to hell.

As the bells continued to toll, the patrons from the surrounding parishes, Saint-Édouard-de-Gentilly, Saint-Gregoire-le-Grand, Le Precieux Sang, La Nativite-de-la-Notre-Dame-de-Becancour, arrived in droves and quietly entered the church, crowding together in each pew. There were too many people for all to be seated comfortably.

Drifting deep in thought my great-grandfather contemplated his duties, the courteous interactions he would have to engage after the mass with the mourners and other visitors. He had always mingled comfortably with friends and families after each funeral mass, offering sympathies and fellowship. But, today, he could not bear it. Celina had been by his side for eighteen years

Elzear remembered his first encounter with Celina, envisioning her beauty, her auburn hair caressing her shoulders, her smooth olive complexion, and her youthful energy. He had been immediately smitten with her. He smiled to himself reminiscing about her mischievous smirk, her witty tongue and the sparkle in her eyes. How easily she became silly and giddy after only a few sips of *piquette*. Full of piss and vinegar. How he already ached for her presence.

How could God expect him to survive without her, to continue to raise a family of nine children, including a two-month-old baby in need of her mother's breast for survival? He would have to persevere, to find the courage to care for his nine children alone. This, I am certain would have tested his mettle. He was a man of great strength and courage and I have always aspired to be like him, to live my life with high moral values and accept what God has chosen for me, without question. My great-grandfather was proud of his heritage and in that moment he knew that he would survive this tragedy. He truly believed that his ancestor's strong will and determination had been passed down to him through many generations and that he had inherited their courage, their strength and their ability to endure, and he would cope with whatever God decided.

Then the stories of Pierre Comeau and Germain Doucet popped in his head. They were Elzear and Celina's ancestors, some of the first European settlers on Acadia soil in the mid 1600s. Both families had married in Port Royal and established long lasting ties in the colony. Their lives had been intertwined since they had first stepped foot in North America. Incredibly, both families had survived the Great Upheaval. Forced to abandon their land in Acadia, they had eluded the British by hiding in the woods and fleeing to Quebec. They had endured tremendous hardships, starvation, sickness, and death, but they had made it to the Becancour region in Quebec.

While reminiscing, Elzear continued pulling on the ropes, still maintaining the rhythm. When Antoine Leblanc tapped him on the shoulder, and startled him, he had become oblivious to the loud ringing and the elapsed time.

"Elzear, that's enough ringing. Everyone is in the church waiting, including Father de Villers."

When Elzear returned from the bell tower to the church, his nine children were waiting for him around their mother's coffin. Two-month-old Marie was fussing in the arms of her eldest sister, Agnes.

Chapter 2

Ste. Gertrude, Quebec – 1869

At Celina's gravesite, Elzear, his friends and family members bowed their heads as Father de Villers read a prayer and sprinkled holy water on her casket. Jean Baptiste Cyr and Antoine Leblanc, his two closest friends, lowered the crate into the ground.

"Grant this mercy, O Lord, we beseech Thee, to Thy servant departed, that she may not receive in punishment the requital of his deeds who in desire did keep Thy will, and as the true faith here united her to the company of the faithful, so may Thy mercy unite her above to the choirs of angels. Through Jesus Christ our Lord."

Everyone responded, "Amen".

Elzear was relieved when the parishioners dispersed quickly after offering their condolences. Close friends had left the church with baskets of bread, fruit pies, and, most importantly, vats of milk for the baby and dropped them off to the girls at home.

It was not the first time that this family was grieving. Year after year, Celina had given birth to girls, five daughters in a row. Then, in 1861, Father Paul de Villers' entry B. 26 in the parish registry read: The twenty-fourth of May, eighteen hundred and sixty-one, I, having signed, have baptized Pierre Joseph, born the same day of the legitimate marriage of Elzear Comeau and Celina Doucet, of this parish. Godfather Leon Champoux, godmother, Ediltrude Tourigny who have signed with us.

Celina had finally given birth to a son. The couple was ecstatic. The little fellow with big brown eyes and dark curls was adored and coddled by his sisters and parents. They felt blessed. Sadly, a few pages later, entry S. 7 recorded his death. He had lived only a few months.

The codes B, M, and S listed alongside an entry in the parish register were to keep track of the baptisms, the marriages, and the burials. The S represented *Sepulture* (burial). As each event happened, Father wrote the names of the deceased, newborns, brides, and grooms in the margin of the booklet along with the code and the code's sequential number. This system made it easy to keep track of the number of events throughout the year. Their son Pierre had been the twenty-sixth child baptized and the seventh death that year. Soon after they buried Pierre, Celina gave birth to another boy, Phileas. Two more boys, Onesiphore and Omer, followed before baby Marie's birth.

Marie was born sickly. Celina's previous babies had all been fat and rosy-cheeked like a Gerber baby, but baby

Marie was pale, gaunt and gangly. Since birth, she had always fussed but not very loudly. Her voice was timid, and her movements slow. It was not for the lack of attention that she fussed, since her older sisters doted on her continually. But, Celina had carried the child while struggling with her illness. The pregnancy had threatened the baby's health and in retrospect the child should never have been conceived in the first place. But through their faith, they believed that a child is God given and they accepted the consequences that came to them.

One morning, a couple of months after Celina had passed away, baby Marie was found dead in her cradle. They had struggled to keep her healthy. Madame Tourigny, a neighbour and dear friend who was nursing a child of her own, would come over almost every day and put Marie to her breast. The fatty milk was like liquid gold to a sick child and provided the best nourishment to get her through the illness, but it did not make a difference. No one knew what malady the child had developed. Doctor Thibodeau had been over many times but could not provide a proper diagnosis. She had a weak immune system, is all he would say. Marie often had trouble breathing and would occasionally gasp for air. Respiratory illnesses were common in infants, especially croup, but her barky cough seemed to indicate a condition much more severe than croup. Agnes had put her to sleep, and sometime during the night she had taken her last breath.

The following month, fourteen-year-old daughter, Ursule, who had so lovingly cared for her mother during her illness, died suddenly.

Poor Elzear! Three graves to dig for his family in just a few months!

Grief-stricken once again Elzear questioned how God expect them to endure all of these deaths? He was sad, heartsick, and numb. The suffering that had never left him since Celina's death had now compounded tenfold. He felt that God was testing him, testing his faith. He knew that when hard times happened, the true nature of his faith would be revealed. He knew his inner emptiness came from a lack of connection with his spiritual leader. So my great-grandfather went to the graveyard to dig another hole and then went to church to pray and receive spiritual guidance from his good friend, Father Paul de Villers.

Like their ancestors in Acadia, the Gertrudians were unwavering in their faith in God. To fulfill their religious duties, they gathered frequently to hear the Scriptures read and to break bread together. In the Becancour region there were more than five parishes, within a fifteen mile radius. It was evident that the Catholic religion was a big part of their lives, and they lived every day to feel God's presence and power. They trusted him with their life more than they trusted themselves; they trusted his timing even when they were running out of patience; they trusted his decisions even when they didn't like them, and they loved him with all their heart even when they didn't understand him.

They all leaned on the church for comfort. The Comeau family and Father De Villers were very well acquainted. The older children often helped their father clean inside the church while the younger children frolicked throughout the grounds and entertained themselves. Their favorite game was playing Holy Communion.

"Virginie, run home and get a small bowl from the kitchen," Lea ordered her younger sister.

Meanwhile, she marched the remainder of the brood to the wild rose bushes growing on the east side of the churchyard. They picked the rose petals and saved them into their pockets until Virginie returned with a bowl. Then Lea lined them up in single file. Acting as Father De Villers, she gently placed a rose petal on their tongues, one by one.

"Corpus Christi," she repeated as each one received pretend communion.

"Amen," they each responded.

"And don't chew it!" She reminded them that it was forbidden to chew the petal.

Father was fond of the children and he tolerated just about any nonsense and sometimes even encouraged it. He was particularly compassionate during their time of grieving and loved to see them happy and smiling. But he had no patience for misbehaving in the cemetery; it was a place for quiet reflection.

Elzear's daughters, aged ten to seventeen, tried desperately to maintain the household to the standard they were accustomed to before their mother passed away. They were determined to do this for their father's sake and their younger siblings. The girls made every effort to mimic their mother's way of doing the chores, the cooking, and arranging the house. They wanted to do everything Celina's way. Keeping themselves busy would help them with the grieving process; keeping things the same would make the days seem normal, like she was still here. It would also help soothe the younger children, so that they wouldn't be reminded of their mother's absence so easily.

The daunting task of maintaining peace and harmony, feeding seven children plus their elderly grandfather Michel, who lived with them in this small house, was proving difficult for the girls. My great-grandfather sensed this and knew that he would soon have to find himself a wife.

Chapter 3

Harry

My mother was alone to welcome me into this world. When I opened my eyes, my father was already deep in the ground in the Bellevue cemetery. My name is Harry Comeau Jr. I was born a posthumous child in Hoey, Saskatchewan, 1930.

When I was young, I remember my Grandmother, Delphine, telling me we were Acadian. I didn't know what that meant and I never asked. Since most of the francophones in the community were French Canadians, I assumed that's what it meant: we were French Canadian, hailing from Quebec. It was much later in my life that I discovered that my roots dated back to Port Royal, Acadia, where my ancestors set foot on North American soil in the mid 1600s. So, I never knew my father, Harry Comeau Sr. and I never knew my grandfather Arthur

Comeau. By the time I began to question my heritage, my Grandmother Delphine, my one aunt and my uncles had all abandoned me. I had lost all my paternal connections. I desperately wanted to know what had influenced my character, my values and my beliefs. Who were my ancestors and what beliefs, ideologies and pleasures did they hold dear to their hearts?

I discovered that many of my ancestors' loves and passions are the same things I enjoyed in my life, the things I held dear to my heart. So while I am telling you this story, many thoughts and emotions from my own life come to mind. When I connect these snippets of my life to my ancestors, it helps me understand who I am as a man. I feel rooted. Perhaps the acorn doesn't fall too far from the tree, even though that tree may have originated long ago, in the seventeenth century.

Every man has a unique story, a history identical to no other, and this is my story. It is about the three-hundred-year journey of my ancestors from Acadia to Saskatchewan. A journey of hardships, endurance, and perseverance. A journey that not only paved the way for my existence but rooted me with a deep affection for my heritage. And how in so many ways it shaped my life, my character and influenced the makeup of my personality.

Now let's go to the beginning...

Chapter 4

Port Royal, Acadia - 1632

Historians believe that there exists only one strain of Comeaus in North America and it is completely Acadian. It doesn't matter how you spell the Comeau name: Comeau with one m or two m's, Comeau ending in eau, eaux or eault, or any of the other forty variations of the name, you are likely a descendant of Pierre Comeau. Pierre was the first Comeau to set foot on Acadian soil and became the ancestral patriarch of all the Comeaus in North America. I am an eight-generation descendant of Pierre Comeau.

In the early 1600s and for more than a century, Acadia (present-day Nova Scotia), was one of the most contested pieces of land in North America. There were continuous wars and bitter struggles between the French and the English. While the English were forever seizing the land, the French were forever bartering to get it back. In 1632, while Acadia was under French rule, France organized an expedition to strengthen their foothold on Acadian soil and begin settling the colony. They were fearful of the British's constant threat of re-seizing the land. Isaac de Razilly, the King's newly appointed governor of Acadia, left France that year with a fleet of three ships and anchored on the south shore of Acadia at LaHève (present day LaHave, Nova Scotia). In addition to the sailors and soldiers on board, Razilly had recruited three-hundred tradesmen. Amongst these skilled workers were artisans and craftsmen, elite men so to speak, all hand-picked by Razilly himself. Pierre Comeau was one of them.

Most of the passengers on Razilly's expedition were from the coastal regions of Brittany, Normandy, Picardy, and Poitou. They had left their home country in search of a more peaceful life. Their homeland had suffered great hardships in the late sixteenth and early seventeenth centuries, as a series of wars between the Catholics and the Protestant Huguenots brought on famine and social tensions. Huguenots were French Protestants who followed the teachings of theologian John Calvin. They were severely persecuted in France, often given the choice of death or conversion to Catholicism. Many fled their country. In a short period of time, more than 10,000 people left France for England, Germany, New France, Acadia, and British North America. Unsure of Pierre's origin in France, historians believe he came from the Poitou region and was a Huguenot. While most men in France were directly employed in agriculture, very few Huguenots were farmers. They were professional people, artisans, and designers, revered for their craftsmanship. They had a reputation for being stubborn.

At the port of LaHève, Razilly and his group of men built a habitation consisting of his residence, a store, a chapel, and a fort, Fort Sainte-Marie-de-Grâce. Once the settlement of LaHève was well underway, Razilly sent some of the men, including Pierre Comeau, to Port Royal to restore the fort. It had been destroyed by the English in 1613 when they had control of Acadia.

Under French rule, Port Royal flourished and became one of the oldest settlements in North America. At this settlement in 1649, Pierre Comeau, aged fifty-one, married eighteen-year-old Rose Bayon, and they settled on a piece of farmland located east of the fort on the south shore of the Dauphin River. They were amongst some of the first Acadians to establish a small, vibrant colony around the Bay of Fundy and together became the ancestral patriarch and matriarch of the Acadian Comeau family.

However, they were not the first inhabitants of the region. The Mi'kmaq people had lived here for more than ten thousand years. The two groups quickly formed a friendship that proved very advantageous. During their first winter, the Acadians suffered great hardships. They were unfamiliar with the harsh climate, and many died from famine and scurvy. But they had the willingness to learn from the Mi'kmaq and this knowledge significantly improved their survival rate. They fared much better in the second winter. The Acadians learned how to use snowshoes, and toboggans, build canoes and navigate the waters; this gave them independence and a way to communicate easily with their neighbours. They were taught to brew pine needles and make a tea high in Vitamin C to ward off scurvy. In exchange, the Acadians introduced the Christian faith, schools, and new European technologies to the Mi'kmaq. The two cultures became intertwined; they engaged in social gatherings, intermarried, and their children attended school together. Their bond was crucial to their survival, and they had a very amicable and peaceful relationship for many, many years.

When the Acadians first arrived in North America they discovered salt march hay, called Spartina along the bay. It grew naturally despite the tides that covered it twice daily. They developed a water control system, a system of draining ditches combined with a one-way water gate called an *aboiteau*. This allowed the lands to desalinate over a few years, making them entirely fertile for crop production. This undertaking earned them the nickname *défricheurs d'eau*, or clearers of water. It became essential for the stability and self-sufficiency of their communities. As a result, the Acadian's standard of living, while laborious and rigorous, became greatly enhanced very rapidly.

~~~~~~

It has been questioned many times: why would the Acadians prefer to dike the marshes rather than clear forests on higher ground? Some speculate that this was a genuine characteristic of the Acadians: it represented their stubbornness or perhaps their ingenuity. Historically, tensions over land ownership between European settlers and Indigenous groups have always existed, however, this conflict never occurred in Acadia. As expert dyke-builders, they were physically creating much of the land they occupied rather than clearing and overtaking Indigenous lands. Ingenuity at its best and perhaps the only reason the two groups co-existed peacefully and developed a relationship that was very rare in colonial era North America. There were never any battles, disputes or bloodshed over land. Now bring in the English and you have a completely different story!

Historians also believe that no other group in North America developed settlements based on the reclamation of salt marshes. The *aboiteau* system, the one way gate system they developed, would become a symbol of Acadian heritage.

Pierre farmed and was a cooper: a professional barrel maker. He was a highly skilled artisan, a craftsman trained to produce barrels of all types. It was a very specialized trade that required ingenuity, intelligence, and strength. The construction of a barrel was from beginning to end completed by an individual cooper; a one-man, one-barrel method. Each cooper developed their unique techniques, styles, and tools of the trade; the skills were taught, shared, and passed down from father to son. It is not difficult to understand why Pierre had been chosen as one of Razilly's elite men to accompany him to Acadia.

Port Royal quickly became a busy metropolis, thriving with professional men: Jean Pitre, an edge tool maker,

Antoine Hebert, Jacques Belou, and Pierre Lanoie, were all coopers like Pierre, Clement Betrand and Thomas Cormier, carpenters, Jacques Bourgeois, a surgeon, Pierre Doucet, a bricklayer, Abraham Dugast and Pierre Sire, gunsmiths, Pierre Melancon, a tailor. These were some of Razilly's elite men who were instrumental in providing for the societal needs of Acadia. It was a very close-knit community of French immigrants who had arrived in Acadia at approximately the same time. They shared work, goals, and interests.

There were several coopers in Port Royal at this time because of the huge demand for these vessels. Many foods, especially those that needed long-term storage, were placed in barrels: fermented cabbages, fish, meats, and eggs. The barrels protected the food from vermin and could be packed between layers of straw to keep them cooler. In addition, the smaller crafted casks stored wine, milk, flour, gunpowder, and tobacco.

The Acadians often repurposed used barrels for washtubs and buckets. Barrels cut in half also made a great cradle. With a new baby arriving almost every year in Pierre and Rose's house, it was common to find a barrel-made cradle parked in the main living area of their house.

The group of Acadian coopers often gathered to socialize and discuss the trade. Jacques and Antoine, two of Pierre's colleagues dropped into his cooperage one afternoon.

"Pierre, we hear you have acquired something special... a new tool?" Jacques commented.

"Look at this precisely crafted barrel," Antoine remarked.

They examined a barrel Pierre had just finished and commented on the precision of the staves. They considered it perfection. They were intrigued. Pierre was happy to see his friends and excited to demonstrate his new tool.

"*Eh, oui.* Come and see! I will show you how it works, and then you can try it for yourself. It certainly makes the job a lot easier."

His newest possession was a drawing compass, a necessary tool of the trade to help him create perfect circles, smooth curves, and arcs. They all had the standard tools of the trade: adzes, axes, jointer and irons, carpenters and cooper's bits, vices, augers, gimlets which their good friend, Jean Pitre had manufactured for them. However, a drawing compass was the tool they most desired, but most did not have it in their arsenal. Antoine and Jacques were envious of Pierre and anyone fortunate enough to procure one.

Pierre continued to make casks and barrels into his eighties. He thoroughly enjoyed working with wood and metal, but most of all he treasured the kinship and the camaraderie he had established with the other local coopers.

By 1671, the settlement of Port Royal had a population of 441, consisting of 68 families. Pierre Comeau was a hardworking and productive man who owned six arpents of land (five acres), which was a good average compared to the other farmers in the area. He maintained sixteen cows and twenty-two sheep, giving him a fair revenue.

Pierre and Rose raised nine children; although life was busy for them, it was a bucolic lifestyle, a pleasant country environment without many stresses or worries.

Chapter 5

Harry

Discovering that my 5th great-grandfather, Pierre, used a drawing compass three hundred years before me, piqued my curiosity. Drawing, drafting, designing and developing new ideas were some of my favourite pastimes.

As a young boy, I was very interested in how things worked, new inventions, and the world in general. Oh, how I anticipated the arrival of my favourite magazines in the mail. The subscriptions to Popular Mechanics and the Science Mechanics magazines I received every month were exciting and informative and I spent many long winters reading and re-reading each issue until I had absorbed every article. But *Le Monde Colonial Illustre* was my favourite. It was a French review publication, like a modern day National Geographic magazine, with all the magnificent photos, and stories from around the globe, but in black and white. For a young man living in small town Hoey, Saskatchewan, with limited access to the outside world it was a fascinating read. Places I had never heard of before like Madagascar, Tunisia, Cameroon, Myanmar and Tanganyika revealed stories of expeditions, giant turtles, and baby zebras. What young man wouldn't be thrilled to read articles about sheep herding in *la Nouvelle Zealande* (New Zealand), fishing in *La Reunion*, a small French island in the Indian Ocean, or the two page article about the month long visit to Morocco organized by the Touring Club of France, complete with photos of palm trees, Moorish architecture and decorative Arab palaces.

These magazines inspired me to dream about new places. They set the travel bug that smoldered inside me for the rest of my life. They helped me become self-reliant, a self-starter, a keener and they ignited my passion for my creative and design endeavours.

The first invention I put to paper was a braking system to assist a vehicle in stopping when icy conditions existed. By engaging a hand lever, like a parking brake lever, spikes would be released around the tires, piercing into the ice and slowing the vehicle to a halt. I developed the idea after seeing ice cleats for boots. Unfortunately, patents were never issued, and prototypes were never developed. I didn't know if it would work, but it kept my mind occupied with creative thought and my hands busy drawing.

My most significant project was designing and building a tent trailer that accommodated my big family of seven children. It had two fold-out double beds, a couch, and a banquette table that would also convert into double beds. The project was a massive undertaking. We had some great adventures and created terrific memories of travelling with this trailer.

Along with being resourceful, I was very analytical and mathematical. I loved geometry. Calculating rises and threads for stairs and building them never posed a problem for me. I enjoyed modifying my farm equipment for maximum efficiency and ergonomics, including rebuilding the platform and the stairs on one of my combines. The factory design was just not good enough as far as I was concerned.

Let me tell you about my tools. I had many. It was my obsession. If there was a tool available to help me accomplish a task, I had it. If not, I would configure one or invent one. Mechanical, carpentry, electrical, drafting, plumbing, masonry, auto body, and welding tools are just a few that I kept multiples of in my shop.

Many know me for *mes petits papiers*, my little pad of paper I always carried with me. The pad was neatly tucked into a pocket protector along with a pen and a packet of Wrigley's gum. All of my shirts required a breast pocket; it was my signature style, my uniform so to speak, because I would have felt naked without my notepad. I never left the house without it. It was handy to jot down my ideas as they came to mind, important notes, and my shopping list.

Chapter 6

Port Royal, Acadie – 1680

By 1680, the second generation of Comeaus, were married and busy creating families of their own. Etienne, Pierre the eldest, and Jean, the eldest farmed and continued to prosper in the Port Royal area. Marie, the youngest daughter and married at age thirteen, was living in the Pisiguit area, approximately two-hundred miles away. Three children remained at home: Pierre, the youngest, Antoine, and Jean, the youngest. Both the matriarch mother, Rose, and eldest daughter, Francoise, had passed away.

The second son, Pierre the eldest, was well-established in the Port Royal area. He had married Jeanne Bourg, and they farmed on their land east of the fort along the south shore of the Dauphin River, a short distance from the original Comeau homestead. Pierre and Jeanne started their family immediately, and by age forty-six, Jeanne had given birth to eighteen children, including a set of twin girls. Their last child, born in 1705, survived only for a few weeks.

~~~~~~

Like Jeanne, my mother gave birth to me when she was almost forty-six years old. If you think that it is uncommon for women to give birth in their forties, think again. Before the early twentieth century, advanced maternal age was not an aberration; it was the norm, with the average age at last birth ranging from thirty-eight to forty-two years old. Unlike Pierre and Jeanne's family, ours was small. With my mother's late start in getting married combined with my father's death at such a young age, there was just my brother and me.

Pierre the eldest and his younger brother, also named Pierre were six years apart and loved to fish. It was not uncommon for younger Pierre to set out early in the morning to his older brother's house for the day to help him with his farming. But most of the time it was to lure him out into the boat for a day of fishing.

"Eh Pierre, are we going fishing today?" called Pierre the youngest, entirely out of breath from running a few miles up the road to his older brother's farm.

"*Bien sur*," Pierre the eldest replied, motioning to get the nets and rods.

They were both excellent at catching fish. Pierre, the eldest, had earned the nickname of sturgeon or big fish because he was incredibly skilled at harvesting large fish: trout, salmon, and sturgeon. Sometimes he would snag a small shark on his line.

Each year in the early part of May, hundreds of thousands of *gaspereaus* (known as Alewife, a type of herring) made their way inland, swimming against the current, leaping through rapids and teeming in shallow pools. Pierre, the eldest, navigated the boat close to one of these shallow pools, and within seconds Pierre, the youngest, caught hundreds of fish with his bare hands, filling the boat in record time. It was breathtaking to watch.

"*Ah, c'est ci bon la peche aujoud'hui; les poissons sont abondants*," voiced young Pierre enthusiastically, "great fishing today; the fish are plentiful."

"I will drop you off at home after we lay the fish to dry at Ile aux Chevres (Goat Island)," said Pierre the eldest.

This tiny island across from Port Royal was the perfect spot to dry the fish. All the locals used it. Long before the island came into view, they inhaled the briny, pungent smell of the salty fish left to dry in the sun. At times they were hard-pressed to find a piece of rock free of fish. Once the little *gaspereaus* were laying on the rock, soaking up the sun like a crowded beach on the Florida coast at spring break, the two Pierres headed home.

Pierre, the youngest, had been given the nickname *Loups-Marins*, meaning sea wolf or seal. He was a great seal hunter and had mastered the sounds of the seals. His high-pitched bleats mimicking the cries of a seal pup was his trademark and recognizable by everyone in the community. Both Pierres were master anglers, providing an abundance of fish for their families.

~~~~~~

Hunting and fishing were some of the hobbies I enjoyed early on in life. In the early sixties, my brother Andy and I created Comeau Construction Co. Ltd., a road-building company that operated massive earth-moving equipment. While contracted to build roads in northern Saskatchewan, we were able to fish many virgin lakes, not readily accessible to the public. The opportunity to experience our province's pristine lakes, rivers, and untouched landscapes are memories forever etched in my mind. From La Ronge, we built a gravel road to Missinipe and north to McLennan Lake. Today, Saskatchewanians can access and enjoy some truly spectacular lakes in the north because of this road.

I have fond memories of this venture, being an earth mover. It was exhilarating to operate heavy machinery: Euclid scrappers, Wagner tractors, and bulldozers, some weighing over fifteen thousand pounds, almost twenty feet in length, and with tires over five feet tall. I also loved farming. And like my ancestors it was a natural fit for me. So when I used this massive equipment in the field for farming, more than just the neighbouring farmers came to gawk!

It didn't take long for Pierre and Jeanne to become self-sufficient on their farm. They grew oats, wheat, barley and planted huge gardens of turnips, beets, carrots, cabbages, salad greens, and herbs. They raised cattle, sheep, chickens and pigs. Pigs were so numerous, they commonly roamed freely in the yards, and were rarely counted when enumerators came around. The pork was their primary source of protein. They preferred to save the cattle for trading, to utilize them as working animals, and for milk. Of course, hunting and fishing also supplemented their diet.

Jeanne and her daughters baked bread daily, a staple of the Acadian diet. In addition, they planted many fruit trees, pears, apples, and plums, purchased mostly from English merchants. Fruit pies, jams, and fruit cakes often included molasses, raisins and brown sugar, ingredients available because of the commerce between Acadia and regions like the Antilles.

The young ladies spent the long winters busy carding wool that had been sheared earlier in the year and spinning it into cloth. They particularly liked the colours of black and red for their garments and would often pull out the red threads from discarded English cloth one by one to brighten their handiwork. They sat around the warm fire knitting, sewing, and tanning beaver pelts and moose hides for moccasins and harnesses. They made soap and candles. From the feathers of ducks, they created beautiful eiderdown comforters and mattresses. These were some of the only luxuries they enjoyed for comfort. The fowl were revered as much for their feathers as for their eggs and meat and the Acadian women became known for their down duvets and coverlets.

Meanwhile, the men kept busy hunting and tending to the animals. When the sap ran in the spring, they made maple syrup and brewed their spruce and fir beer. The entire family pitched in to ensure that the food supply was always plentiful and that everyone was well-fed and clothed.

Trade goods of wine, brandy, fruit trees, molasses, sailcloth and French linens arrived periodically on barges from Boston to the shores of the Bay of Fundy. In exchange for grain, feathers, and furs they had acquired from the Mi'kmaq, the Acadians enhanced their lifestyle immensely.

After a few prosperous years, the Comeau siblings had collectively acquired one hundred and thirty-five acres of land, seventy-five cows, forty-one hogs, one hundred and twenty-two sheep, and several firearms. In addition, they nurtured and cared for more than one-hundred and fifty fruit trees on their properties. Their life was a hard one, but a simple and good one. They lived in a harsh landscape, but they made it work for them.

Meanwhile, the English and the French continued to fight over Acadia. During this period the English were sometimes their friends and sometimes they were their enemies – *nos amis, les enemis*. The Acadians, forced to play both sides by necessity, soon developed a fondness for their simple way of life. Until 1755, they lived fairly contently.

Before the turn of the eighteenth century, Pierre, the patriarch of the North American Comeau bloodline, had passed away. Left behind were seven children, fifty-four grandchildren, and twenty great-grandchildren, all living in nearby Port Royal, except Antoine. Antoine had mysteriously disappeared!

Chapter 7

Harry

Have you ever wondered why families had multiple children with the same name? In Pierre and Rose's family there were three Pierres; the father named Pierre, and the sons, Pierre, the eldest and Pierre, the youngest. There were also two Jeans and a Jeanne. How confusing! It seems ridiculous to me that two children in the same family would be given the same name. However, in the seventeenth-century names like Pierre and Jean were very common. They had a habit of recycling the names of their beloved kinfolk: their grandfather, their father, their father's eldest brother, their mother's father, etc., so they would often end up with multiples of the same name over three or four subsequent generations. Duplicate names used were often succeeded by *l'aine,* the eldest, or *le jeune,* the youngest, similar to Sr. and Jr. Sometimes they would attach a nickname, as was the case for Pierre and Pierre. Pierre, the eldest, was also known as *l'Esturgeon*, the Sturgeon or Big Fish. Pierre the youngest's nickname was *Loups-Marins*, meaning Sea Wolf or seal. I am sure one of the Pierres would have been named after his father! I was also fortunate to be named after my father.

Similarly, it was also common to re-use the name of a child that had not survived very long. For people researching their genealogy, or trying to tell a story, this could be quite challenging and confusing.

Can you imagine my poor 5th great-grandmother, Rose, hollering for a Pierre or a Jean? Three Pierres and two Jeans in the same household; *c'est absurd*.

Chapter 8

Chipoudie, Acadie - 1730

The Acadians had developed a peaceful lifestyle with few maladies or life-threatening diseases. There were no significant food shortages for over two decades, nor any major epidemic of measles, chickenpox, or smallpox. While seventy-five percent of Acadians reached adulthood, during this same period in France, only fifty percent reached the age of twenty-one.

With the birth rate very high and the child mortality rate very low, the Acadian population multiplied quickly and between 1730 and 1750, Acadia was known as the Golden Age. Gradually newer generations of Acadians migrated east and north to areas where land was more abundant. They scattered along the shores of the three rivers that emptied into the Bay of Fundy: the Petitcodiac, the Memramcook, and the Chipoudie Rivers. Tiny fishing settlements and farming communities were quickly established, stretching from present-day Amherst, Nova Scotia, west to the communities of Shepody, Hopewell Hill and Riverside Albert, and eventually north to Moncton in New Brunswick.

The second generation of Comeaus, Pierre the eldest, and Jeanne Bourg's children, were amongst the early settlers in the Chipoudie region. Of their eighteen children, fourteen survived to establish families in Acadia with twelve siblings settling in this new area. Among the siblings was Francois Comeau, the fifteenth child, married to Anne Lord in 1724. The Lords had farmed directly across the Comeau marshes on the north side of the Annapolis River at Port Royal, a short canoe ride across the water. So the Comeaus and the Lords grew up together, and it was inevitable that some of the children would marry. Five of the Lord's children married into the Comeau family over several generations.

Francois and his brother, Jean, took up properties along the Chipoudie River, located near present-day Riverside-Albert, NB. Directly across the river, four of Francois' young nephews were farming. Other brothers Joseph, Maurice, and Ambroise, along with sister Marie, (married to Claude Pitre), were all farming three miles east at Hopewell, NB. This entire area was known as Village-des-Jeunes-Comeau, (Village of the young Comeaus) and Prés-des-Comeau, (Comeau meadows).

The Thibodeaus and Blanchards were the original settlers to this area in the late 1690s. Two of Francois's sisters were married to Thibodeau sons and were situated near-by at present day Hopewell Hill, NB. Other

Comeaus who married into Blanchard families were located north along the west shore of the Petitcodiac River near present-day Hillsborough.

Life was not easy for the first few years in Chipoudie. Like the newly arrived settlers in Port Royal, they had to clear the land, grow crops, and build shelters. Their lands were occupied without authorization and few settlers possessed the paperwork to identify they had a legal hold on the plots. Boundaries were never established; they farmed side by side, sharing the work and the harvest.

As difficult as life started out in Chipoudie, Francois and Anne were content raising their nine children. Famine, disease, and war had barely touched them, and they quickly prospered. It was a joyous time. Although it was hard work to get established, there was always sufficient food for the growing families and enough new land for the ever-increasing population.

Near their home, the community had built a little chapel, which they named Notre Dame de la Visitation, where the locals congregated every Sunday for camaraderie, fellowship and prayer. After the service they gathered outside on the church grounds called *champs commus* or common fields. The men discussed their crops, farming, hunting, and fishing while the women socialized and the children played. Often, they brought food and enjoyed a communal picnic. The Catholic religion played an essential role in the lives of the Acadians.

By the early 1750s, twenty-eight Comeau families had sprouted in the region. Their society consisted of closely-knit families who depended on each other socially and economically, and this cooperation helped maintain their culture. Music and song were an important part of their culture, and they indulged in sing-songs and dancing to occupy their long winter evenings. They also engaged in card-playing, pipe-smoking, as well as story-telling. When spring and summer emerged, the celebrations of weddings and new births were a welcoming change. My ancestors were outgoing people and enjoyed social gatherings.

"*Chez nous, demain soir*," (our place, tomorrow night!), yelled Francois to his brother, Jean, across the meadow. "Let everyone know that we are having a gathering tomorrow night at our house."

It was a familiar invitation, a cause to celebrate. Every year there were multiple weddings to celebrate amongst the Comeau families, and 1752 was no exception. Tomorrow's occasion was the wedding of Francois and Anne's daughter, Marie Anne, to Louis Rousse. The sky was promising a perfect July day, and the wedding was a magnificent opportunity for an Acadian-style party. Often with the consumption of alcohol, homemade spruce beer, cider, and rum, the party would begin with music and dancing.

The next morning the Chapel's bells rang loud throughout Chipoudie. It was the familiar call for celebration that everyone recognized. The morning wedding was a happy occasion and just a brief greeting afterward ensured everyone was back to work before lunch. By late afternoon all the relatives, neighbours and friends gathered at the Comeau meadows with food and beverage in hand. They came in droves carrying armloads of hot pots containing fried clams, fish cakes, *fricot* (chicken and dumplings), *bouilli acadien* (stew or boiled dinner of potatoes, salted pork, carrots, cabbage, and other vegetables). They carried pie plates of *tourtieres* (meat pies), sugar pies, fruit pies and dishes of sweet *pouding chomeur* (poor man's pudding) and apple dumplings smothered in maple syrup. The children lugged baskets containing loaves of bread and pancakes while the men transported the beer, cider, rum, and wine. What a celebration!

"*Allons-y*," shouted the younger Comeaus in unison, clapping their hands and pounding their feet to the music made by the older generation.

"Get the spoons out," called Francois to his kids.

The Acadian party had started with reel bouche music, as they called it; it was nonsense syllables they made with their mouths to imitate the sounds of other instruments. And the wooden or metal spoons were knocked together to create percussion accompaniment to the music. The lively skipping, stepping and heel-toe tapping movement, a distinct dance similar to a jig, clogging or a hoedown, was so fast that everyone's feet were a blur! They sang their favourite song:

Zigue, zigue, zon, zon, zeux
Allons-y a la riviere
Avec l'eau si bleu
Pour y attraper
Un gros poisson visqueux
Pour ma soeur si belle
Sa va la rendre folle

Et faires ses jambres si molles,
Ah, c'est si drole, ce jeux
Zigue, zigue, zon, zon, zeux

~~~~~~

Ah! *Un party d'cuisine.* The memories of the Acadian wine, whisky, and moonshine-soaked kitchen parties; the musical traditions of non-stop fiddling, singing and jigging! I remember them well. I loved a good Acadian party; well, any party for that matter. I was a very social person and created bonds and friendships easily with everyone.

My uncles came to Saskatchewan to visit us in the late 1950s. My uncle Norman was from Quebec, and my uncle Clarence came from Massachusetts. My aunt Ena, who had passed away at age forty-one giving birth to her tenth child, had created a large family with her husband. They were the Ethiers', nine cousins, living nearby with their spouses. It created a huge Acadian party! With the lively music from the fiddles, spoons, and whatever else we could find to clang together, the Comeaus always partied till the wee hours of the morning.

These close ties and large families always sparked great get-togethers!

The chapel bells at Notre Dame de la Visitation continued to ring often as more weddings were celebrated and more children were born. By 1755, over sixteen hundred people, more than two hundred families, lived in the three rivers region. The Comeau families accounted for almost twenty-five percent of the population, fifty families and more than two hundred and sixty children. Marie Anne Comeau and her new husband, Louis Rousse, began their family immediately. They would be one of the first Comeaus to leave the area in the summer of 1755 with three young children and make their way to Quebec to begin a new life. Many other Comeaus would follow suit.

But when the chapel bells rang for what would be the very last time, it was not to announce a celebration.

"Francois, Francois!" yelled Father LeGuerne, their local missionary, running through the meadows. "The English have been spotted navigating up the Chipoudie River. There is no time left. Alert everyone and evacuate. NOW!"

The bells rang continuously for a long time. It alerted everyone working in the marshes; everyone knew what it meant. They were terrified. They knew the British soldiers were coming to round them up and expel them from their lands. They were coming to torch their homes and church, slaughter their animals, destroy their crops and seize their land.

Chapter 9

Match in the Powder-Barrel - 1754

It is shocking to think of how many battles were fought over the possession of Acadia between the French and the English during the first eighty years of its existence. In peacetime, the English came to trade; they were friends. In war, they came to conquer; they were enemies. In 1613 the English attacked and burned Port-Royal. They attacked again in 1629. Then, in 1654, they captured Port-Royal and controlled the territory until France regained it by treaty in 1670. The English attacked again in 1690, 1704, and 1707. The colony of Acadia changed hands at least ten times between 1604 and 1710.

From the very start of English dominance over the territory, there had always been one matter of constant irritation for the British: the Acadians' refusal to pledge loyalty to the English Crown. The Acadians were continually harassed to sign an oath of allegiance to the King, but they just wanted to be left alone, undisturbed, and in peace, regardless of who controlled the colony. Instead, they wanted to remain neutral. They were the second, third and fourth generations of Acadians who had never lived in France, so they had no allegiance to France either. And France had always ignored them and left them to fend for themselves. For this reason, they became very independent-minded. They had no desire to bend the knee and pledge loyalty to France or England. They felt secure with their friends and allies, the Mi'kmaq, and when sovereignty over their land passed back and forth from Britain to France and vice versa, they believed it would continue indefinitely. So why pledge their allegiance when they would be making a promise to a government that might not be around for long?

While this continual back-and-forth change of hands occurred, the Acadian boundaries were never correctly assigned. Most of the time the undefined territory included the land east of New England and Southeast of New France and sometimes even parts of Maine. The Isthmus of Chignecto, which connects Nova Scotia to North America, was the river that the French and the English arbitrarily adopted as the official boundaries between Nova Scotia and New Brunswick. Both powers built rival garrisons here: Fort Lawrence and Fort Beausejour. They were separated only by the river and a mile of marshes. In peacetime, the two sides exchanged civilities, and during wartime, they exchanged shots across the river. More than any other location in Acadia, the Chignecto region experienced the greatest number of attacks and raids.

Each time the territory changed hands, a new Governor was appointed or a new King was crowned, and the Acadians were pestered to sign an oath. It was a constant annoyance that they mostly ignored or declined. They were notoriously stubborn and refused to accept the demands for allegiance to Britain or France. Their unwillingness to sign an oath tested the British's patience beyond the limit; it was the match in the powder barrel, the eventual breaking point for the British.

~~~~~~

There is a saying we've all heard before: stubborn as a mule. But have you ever heard the expression stubborn as an Acadian? The story of Acadians has been one of stubborn survival in the face of hardship because they were fiercely protective of their heritage. They have been portrayed as strong, healthy, virtuous people, sincerely attached to their religion, language and traditions. They were stubborn, always enthusiastic to discuss or argue their positions, but never willing to surrender to their beliefs.

Stubbornness is a trait that I recognize in myself and most of my relatives. It has always been difficult, if not impossible, for anyone to change my conviction, attitude, or position on a subject that I firmly believe in, even in spite of good arguments or reasons to do so.

But as stubborn as we are, sometimes we have to give in just to maintain peace.

The British succeeded in obtaining Acadian signatures a few times. One instance was when the oath granted them all of the privileges of citizenship, including the free exercise of their religion which was at that time not afforded to Catholics in Great Britain. And another time when a provision in the oath exempted them from bearing arms, something that appealed to them because they wanted to remain neutral. They gathered outside the Chapel Notre Dame de la Visitation after mass one Sunday to discuss this important matter.

"They are again asking for our signatures," cited Francois's brother, Jean. "I have heard from the other communities that they plan to include a clause in the oath that will excuse us from bearing arms during the skirmishes. In other words, we will pledge our loyalty, but we won't have to fight on either side."

"Is this possible?" asked Charles Thibodeau.

"Yes, I think so. Many communities have already signed," Francois piped in. "You know this won't be the end of it, but at least with this provision identified in the oath, we can avoid any conflict when another war erupts."

"We should be unified," added Jean Comeau. "If everyone else agrees to sign, we should also sign the oath."

The Acadians were skeptical about signing an oath. They never truly believed that signing an oath would bring them peace, or that the British would leave them alone. Because of this prolonged discourse, both sides lacked the confidence to trust each other fully.

~~~~~~

I would have rolled my eyes, or raised a skeptical eyebrow at the signing of an oath. Since it had been a contentious issue for the British for so many years, who could trust them?

The expression 'raise an eyebrow' evokes a state of confusion, surprise, fear, disbelief, or disapproval. When you experience these emotions, raising both eyebrows is a common, unconscious reaction. But much less common is the ability to raise only one eyebrow. Very few people can do this, but I could do it quite easily; my raised eyebrow resembled a circumflex, aka *un petit chapeau* (a little hat), the French accent found on any of the five vowels. Literally, I could arch one eyebrow so high that it looked like an upside-down V.

And I always preferred to raise an eyebrow at someone rather than give them the stink eye; it was more comical and less judgmental. This always amused my children. Could I have inherited this ability from my Acadian ancestors? I imagine that being continually harassed to sign an oath would have become very tiresome and eventually caused them to raise an eyebrow, scowl, or at the very least roll their eyes at the request.

Reluctantly in 1730 many Acadians took an oath of allegiance to the King of England. They promised that as Christians they would be entirely loyal, and truly obedient to His Majesty King George the second, and recognize him as the sovereign Lord of Nova Scotia or Acadia.

With this oath, the Acadians believed they had found a way to protect themselves from participating in the constant wars while preserving their religion and language. From this time forward, the French and the English referred to them as "les francais neutres" or the Neutral French. The Acadians were now recognized as neutral, neither aligned with France nor Britain, which pleased them.

The British became threatened and fearful of the Acadian's relationship with the Mi'kmaq and believed that some favoured the French. When the English conquered Fort Beausejour, Lieutenant Governor Charles Lawrence found Acadians aligned with the Mi'kmaq and discovered more than 270 Acadian militia among the fort's inhabitants.

When the Seven Years' War erupted in 1754, the British government demanded that Acadians take another oath of allegiance to the Crown that included fighting against the French. Again, the Acadians refused. The oath would become the irritation that stretched Lawrence's patience beyond the limit; it would be the straw that broke the camel's back.

At his wit's end, Lawrence prepared to take drastic action. He devised a plan to deport them, scattering them throughout the thirteen British Colonies. Doing so would solve three contentious issues:

1. They would remain British subjects;

2. Distributing them throughout the thirteen colonies would dilute the population, ensuring they would never have sufficient numbers to form a resistance against the British Crown;

3. Finally, their fertile lands in Acadia could be seized and given to the English people.

When he proposed his idea to his chief advisors, they all praised him and said it was an ingenious plan. On August 11, 1755, Governor Lawrence gave his council the expulsion orders. The order stated in part:

'...to come to the Resolution of sending away the French Inhabitants and clearing the whole Country of such bad subjects, it only remains for me to give you the necessary orders for the putting in practice what has been so solemnly determined.

That the Inhabitants may not have it in their power to return to this Province nor to join in strengthening the French of Canada in Louisbourg; it is resolved that they shall be dispersed among his Majesty's Colonies upon the Continent of America.

...

And you will in these orders make it a particular injunction to the said Masters (ship's masters) to be as careful and watchful as possible during the whole course of the passage to prevent the passengers making any attempt to seize upon the vessel by allowing only a small number to be upon the decks at a time and using all other necessary precautions to prevent the bad consequence of such attempts; and that they be particularly careful that the Inhabitants carry no arms nor other offensive weapons on board with them at their embarkation.

...

You will use all the means proper and necessary for collecting the people together so as to get them on board.

If you find that fair means will not do with them, you must proceed by the most vigorous measures possible, not only in compelling them to embark, but in depriving those who shall escape of all means of shelter or support by burning their houses and destroying everything that may afford them the means of subsistence in the country, and if you have not force sufficient to perform this service, Colonel Winslow at Mines or the Commanding Officer there will upon your application send you a proper reinforcement.'[1]

~~~~~~

Like my Acadian forefathers, I would have chosen neutrality: refusing to side with either France or England; refusing to fight, period! I have never liked conflict. The Acadians were kind, loving, and inclusive people. They wanted to live peacefully. For over one hundred and fifty years, they developed a culture based on mutual respect and caring for one another, regardless of race or stature, the same fundamental values that the Mi'kmaq held dearly. Their communities prospered because they believed in fair trading, sharing the land and possessions. Unlike the English, who believed they could only achieve success and prosperity by conquering the land and seizing the inhabitant's possessions. How can anyone fault them for choosing neutrality?

Chapter 10

Le Grand Derangement – 1755

When the French's blue silk cloth with three yellow fleurs-de-lis was snapping in the wind, the colony was called Acadia or L'Acadie. When the British flag, the Union Jack, sporting the colours of red, white, and blue, flew over the colony, the land was known as Nova Scotia. Strangely, it had been named Nova Scotia (New Scotland) by a Scottish King who had inherited the English throne for a very brief time. It would remain known as Nova Scotia for all time.

With the Treaty of Utrecht in 1713, the patriotic cloths changed hands for the last time and France gave possession of the land to England. It remained under British rule until Canada became its own country. So, it was, in fact, the British flag that flapped in the wind in 1755 when the Great Upheaval, the deportation of the Acadians began.

An anonymous letter of August 1755, sent from Halifax to Boston set the tone for a series of events that would destroy the colony of Acadia. It was published throughout the colonial newspapers of New York, Pennsylvania and Maryland.

'We are now upon a great and noble scheme of sending the neutral French out of this Province, who have always been secret enemies, and have encouraged our Savages to cut our throats. If we effect their expulsion, it will be one of the greatest things that ever the English did in America; for by all accounts, that part of the country they possess, is as good land as any in the World: In case therefore we could get some good English farmers in their room this Province would abound with all kinds of provisions.'[2]

~~~~~~

Can you imagine how terrified the Marylanders, New Yorkers and Pennsylvanians would have been after reading the front page news describing the Acadians as "secret enemies who have encouraged our Savages to cut our throats"? Can you imagine how the Acadians would have been received and treated when more than twenty-three hundred arrived at their ports in late 1755 and early 1756?

It's unsure who wrote the letter, but reliable sources attributed it to either Colonel John Winslow, or Governor Charles Lawrence. The tone of the letter is very characteristic of Lawrence's arrogant and sanctimonious personality. Winslow was more sympathetic to the Acadians. Following the orders to remove the Acadians at Grand-Pré, Winslow commented that the act was disagreeable to his nature and temperament. But he carried out his orders as commanded.

The anonymous letter began by arrogantly boasting about the British fleets and how they were prepared to make another attempt on Louisbourg if war should erupt. In 1745, after a forty-nine day siege by the British on Louisbourg, the French surrendered. The news of the capture set off bell-ringing, bonfires, fireworks and singing in the streets of New England, but it was short-lived. The Aix-la-Chapelle treaty in 1748, returned the fort and colony to French control. However, capturing Louisbourg was forever in England's scope; they knew that seizing Louisbourg would pave the way to capture New France and put an end to French rule in North America.

'We make a most grand appearance to our harbour, such a fleet was never before in America; there are eleven sail of line, with several small ships. Admiral Holburn, with six ships is cruising Louisbourg; and Captain Rous with two twenty gun ships and a sloop sailed from hence a few days ago on a secret expedition; 'tis thought to dispossess the French of a small settlement in the westermost part of Newfoundland, where we have heard some vessels from the continent have been so villainous to carry provisions, from whence the French carry it to Louisbourg. Our fleet has taken a Snow bound from France to Cape Breton, loaded with provision; nor will it be possible for any of their vessels to get in while our flee is upon the coast; nor is it unlikely, in case there should be a war, that another attempt would be made on Louisbourg.'[3]

Thus began the Great Expulsion, Le Grand Dérangement, the removal of the Acadian population, an event that continued intermittently for many years during the 1755–1778 period.

The area of Grand-Pré was the first to feel the wrath of the English. On September 5, 1755, Colonel John Winslow, ordered the males in the area, aged ten years and up, to gather in the Grand-Pré Church for an important message from His Excellency, Governor Lawrence. Colonel John Winslow read the decree to the assembled group:

'I have received from his Excellency Governor Lawrence, the King's Commission, which I have in my hand; and by his orders you are convened together to manifest to you, his Majesty's final resolution to the French inhabitants of this his Province of Nova-Scotia; who, for almost half a century, have had more indulgence granted them than any of his subjects in any part of his dominions; what use you have made of it you yourselves best know. The part of duty I am now upon, though necessary, is very disagreeable to my natural make and temper, as I know it must be grievous to you, who are of the same species; but it is not my business to animadvert but to obey such orders as I receive, and therefore, without hesitation, shall deliver you his Majesty's orders and instructions, namely- that your lands and tenements, cattle of all kinds and livestock of all sorts, are forfeited to the Crown; with all other your effects, saving your money and household goods, and you yourselves to be removed from this his Province.'[4]

In simple English, it meant that they would become prisoners, and all their belongings would be forfeited to the British Crown.

Beginning on October 13, 1755, forty ships left the shores of Acadia destined for the British Colonies, carrying more than 7,000 Acadians, half of the population. Hundreds of Acadians were forced into the cargo hold on over-capacity vessels. They encountered heavy storms on the high seas, and with limited food and clean water, many died before arriving at their destination. Family members dispersed throughout Massachusetts, Virginia, the Carolinas, New York, Connecticut, Maryland, Pennsylvania, and Georgia, became separated. Those who survived the journey continued to be ostracized. The colony's administrators were not welcoming and treated them unfairly.

Three thousand others fled into the woods. Four thousand would remain in PEI, Cape Breton, and St. Pierre and Miquelon, French-controlled territory, believing they would be safe from deportation. However, the mass exodus continued ending with the last deportation of St. Pierre and Miquelon in 1778.

This vast influx of Acadian exiles arriving week after week at the British Colony ports was overwhelming for the Administrators. Governor Lawrence had inadequately prepared them; they had not been forewarned of the numbers to be expected or given instructions on what to do with the Acadians. He had sent the paperwork containing the orders for the deportations on the same ships that carried the Acadians into exile, so the Administrators knew nothing in advance. They were surprised when the ships arrived with hundreds of refugees at their ports.

And as the Acadians landed on the shores of Massachusetts to Georgia, each colony coped as best as they could. The exiles posed a problem wherever they went. The authorities were unprepared: Were the deportees to be treated as prisoners of war or as wards of the colony? How were their physical needs to be met? They were a burden to each of the colonies and most certainly not welcomed.

Unfortunately, the Acadians deported to Virginia were refused entry by the Governor. Upon arriving in Williamsburg, they were not allowed to disembark. For four months, they stayed in the harbour in cramped and squalor conditions, where many of them died. Finally, a decision was made. They would be sent to England, to Southampton, Liverpool, Falmouth, and Bristol. They would remain in exile on British soil for seven years, until 1763. Approximately twelve hundred Acadians were rerouted from Virginia to England, arriving in June 1756.

Twenty-six Comeaus were on the ship destined for Bristol.

Just as Governor Lawrence hadn't provided notice to Virginia that the Acadians were coming, Virginia had failed to warn England of the incoming deportees. After being towed up the winding River Avon, the Comeau family's ship remained alongside Bristol Quay for two weeks until a large converted warehouse was found to lodge them. Since they were considered neutrals, they could not be treated as prisoners or placed in prisons.

Shortly after their arrival, the smallpox epidemic spread with terrifying rapidity amongst the four groups. Death from the cold, starvation and other contagious diseases contracted from the squalid conditions in the warehouses were also widespread.

When the Treaty of Paris was signed in 1763, ending the Seven Years' War, the exiled Acadians were free. Only seven hundred and eight-six Acadians remained in England. Of the four hundred and ten exiles who had perished, eleven were Comeaus.

The four groups from Bristol, Falmouth, Liverpool and Southampton expressed their wish to return to Nova Scotia. They asked the King of England to have their possessions restored, indemnities paid for their losses, and be allowed to practice their religion freely. They promised to pledge an oath of fidelity to the English monarchy in return. Lastly, they asked to be exempt from having any fort built among their habitations; they said this would bring them everlasting happiness. They were asking for a lot.

Eventually, all four groups changed their minds. The French Ambassador had secretly sent an advocate from France to visit them and entice them to relocate there. He had outlined a lucrative scheme with the promise of free food, tobacco for three months, gifts of animals, farms, implements, and fifty years' exemption from taxes. The formal promise to settle on lands in France at the expense of the King was too good to resist, and they resolved to accept and be subjects of France. The scheme subsequently ended in disaster.

After seven years exiled in England, the surviving Acadians sailed to St. Malo, France in search of a better life, convinced that France would bring them peace and prosperity. However, France was unfamiliar to them; they had lived their entire lives in Acadia, where they had developed their own culture, heritage, and way of life. France was the beloved land of their ancestors, not theirs. It was a country they were connected with only through their ancestors. Soon they would discover that the promises of a better life had been quite exaggerated.

In France, the Acadian refugees were dependent on the State. Although several projects had been developed to implant them in the coastal regions, they were not very successful. The farmland given to them was of very poor quality and did not provide the promised concessions. Some Acadians settled permanently in the French ports, especially in Bretagne, but most struggled and were very unhappy.

The French government soon realized that the Acadians were becoming a severe drain on the treasury. This burden on France led to the last major migration for these Acadians: Spanish Louisiana. Spain was eager to strengthen its claim in Louisiana and proposed to pay for the transport of any Acadians who wished to leave France and help settle the territory.

The first Acadians had arrived in Louisiana from New York in 1764 after the war had ended. The following year, travelling through Haiti aboard the Santo Domingo, Joseph Broussard, a French Resistance Militia, led two-hundred Acadians from the Halifax detention camps to the Attakapas and Opelousas regions of Louisiana. The Spaniards had immediately welcomed and accepted the Acadian refugees. Once they were settled, many wrote to their families scattered around the Atlantic to invite them to join them in Louisiana. They said, "Come and reunite with fellow Acadians where you can make a good living, in a peaceful land where you will no longer feel threatened by the possibility of war or conflict." Those struggling in France received the invitation and soon joined their fellow Acadians in the Bayou.

Always hoping that life would be better in the next place, many destitute deportees in France took advantage of Spain's offer and left. In 1785, seven ships transported more than 1,600 Acadians from France to Louisiana, their final destination. They arrived in subtropic Louisiana with nothing, but they were immediately welcomed. Louisiana had been populated by immigrants from different regions: American and European whites, African and Carribean slaves. With the addition and mixture of the Acadian culture into the group, they became 'creolized' and are known today as 'Cajuns'.

Once in Louisiana, Acadians whose name ended in the 'o' sound dumbfounded the authorities with their inconsistent spelling. The endings 'eau', 'eault', 'eaux', 'au', 'aux', 'ault', 'ot', 'aut', 'ault' were used interchangeably, but rarely consistently. The Comeaus, Amireaus, Breaus, Bourdeaus, Thibodeau, Robichaud, to name a few, seemed to spell their names as the whim struck them on any given day. Judge Paul Briant of the

St. Martin Parish in charge of the census recognized more than a dozen ways they spelled the sound and found it impossible to keep track. So he arbitrarily selected eaux because he thought it was the most commonly used. Since then, the Cajun Comeaus have spelled their name Comeaux, ending with an 'x'.

From France, other Acadian families were sent to South America to colonize Guiana and the Falkland Islands. In the first group, the rate of mortality was very high; the second group returned to France shortly after. Others began to return to Acadia in the 1770s. However, the majority left France to settle in Louisiana.

The fear and havoc forced many Acadians to leave the land of their birth and flee like fugitives in the woods of New Brunswick. Many crossed the woods under horrible conditions through marshlands and made their way north, where they died in great numbers over the winter from starvation. Others were to wander as exiles in foreign lands for many years, separated from their children and their kin, amongst strangers, speaking a foreign language and practicing a foreign religion. Most of the colonies reluctantly took them in and regarded them as indigents to rescue or enemy prisoners. Having been successful farmers in Acadia, self-sufficient and accustomed to self-governance, they were now penniless and landless. They faced strict and unfamiliar regulations, often discriminatory against Catholics. The more fortunate ones would someday regain their native soil. Of the 14,100 Acadians in the region, approximately 11,500 Acadians were deported.

Sadly when the war finally ended, more than one-half of the Acadian population had perished. At Port Royal, the first Acadian settlement established on Canadian soil, where Acadians had thrived for many generations, only two or three hundred exist there today. Most Acadians never again saw the land where they were born.

~~~~~~

It was like they had gone to bed in their warm houses, families together, with bellies full, and awoke the next morning dispersed all over the world. Like litter, dust and leaves in a violent windstorm, they had been scattered to the four winds.

Chapter 11

Displaced and Rejected – 1756

At the time of the Great Upheaval, an Acadian's fate might have been determined by where they lived, the timing of the deportations, and their planned escape route - if they were lucky enough to have one. The British began the expulsion by targeting certain regions, and fortunately for the large number of Comeaus in Chipoudie, this area was not the first earmarked for deportation.

But the threat soon reached other areas of Acadia. While the spectacle of deportation was unfolding in the Grand Pre area, Acadians in Chipoudie took notice and made plans to flee inland to the forests. Local missionary, Father LeGuerne, began urging the Acadians in the three rivers area (Petitcodiac, Memramcook, and Chipoudie) to escape to New France (Quebec), Île Saint-Jean (Prince Edward Island) or take refuge upstream on the

Miramichi River or Rivière Saint-Jean (St. John River) in New Brunswick. Many took Father's advice and fled.

The bells at Notre Dame de la Visitation in Chipoudie rang for the very last time when the chapel burned to the ground at the hands of the English. Their villages were overtaken, their communities were demolished, and their families were scattered every which way. More than one hundred and eighty buildings were set on fire and destroyed. Nonetheless, two hundred families escaped deportation because of Father LeGuerne's warning. Still, they lost everything they possessed in the process.

Determined to avoid deportation, Francois, his brothers, and their families began to discuss their alternatives should the British attack. Gathering at Comeau meadows the heads of the twenty-seven Comeau families from the area began to discuss their options.

"We have very few good options to consider," Francois's brother, Jean, contended.

"Who is in favour of going to New France?" asked Charles Thibodeau, Francois's brother-in-law. Everyone pipped in simultaneously.

"Not me!"

"Me neither!"

"I'd rather stay and fight or be captured by the British than go all that way."

"It will be an entirely different lifestyle, not what we are accustomed to."

"They won't be welcoming and we may never see Acadia again if we choose to go. It is a very long distance and the unknown scares me."

"It would be a very difficult journey!"

"I agree! I prefer not to go to New France."

They all agreed. Fleeing to New France was not their destination of choice. They believed that going there would be almost as great a sacrifice as being captured by the British. Almost! Going to New France would mean saying farewell to their way of life, their culture and everything they were deeply attached to. It was far away. The journey would be difficult. They would have to endure considerable famine and hardship. They assumed that they would never be able to return to their beloved Acadia, once they were in New France. They had developed such a fondness for their simple lives. Acadia, to them, was Paradise on Earth, and they believed that they would be miserable in New France.

"Ok, ok. Then let's discuss the possibility of going to another part of Acadia, still under French control, where Acadians live," Francois suggested.

"Like Île Saint-Jean or Île Royale?"

"Yes, those are two good options. Île Saint-Jean is much closer and would be considerably more manageable," Jean commented. "Let's start talking about how we could get this big group, all of us, two hundred plus, men, women, and children safely to Île Saint-Jean. We'll have to make concrete plans and divide into groups. But we must make sure we are ready at a moment's notice."

They told their priest they would prefer to go to Île Saint-Jean, where many fellow Acadians had migrated. The island was a French territory, and they believed that while living amongst their people, they could maintain the same way of life.

As soon as they learned that the British were nearby, they fled northeast into the woods. With the help of Mi'kmaq, using cover and concealment techniques, they successfully distanced themselves from the region where the British were relentless in their efforts to capture them. Moving carefully and slowly, it took them several months to reach Baie Verte and cross the channel to Île Saint-Jean.

~~~~~~

My Acadian ancestors and the Mi'kmaq cultures meshed well together. Like a tightly knitted sweater, a Cowichan of grey and brown wool similar to the one my wife knitted for me in the 1960s, with the stitches so strong they could not be easily unravelled. So were these two groups tightly intertwined. They became one, founded on mutual respect, understanding, acceptance and inclusiveness.

The Mi'kmaq protected our ancestors and welcomed many of those who fled by providing a safe haven at a crucial time during the expulsion. These brave Indigenous men and women sheltered us and fought with the Acadians against the British, who were seeking to deport our people. I believe it is the only reason Acadian descendants survived to exist in Atlantic Canada, Quebec, and all the other Provinces across Canada today. For this, I am forever grateful.

In the woods, the refugees were continually conscious and fearful of Lieutenant Governor Lawrence, who had put a price on their heads. It was an exhausting journey, so when they found a suitable location to set up a temporary home, they stayed as long as they felt safe. Then, when they feared the English were closing in on them, they quickly packed up and moved further north or east into the woods, away from Chipoudie.

Maneuvering through the tangled wood and swamp, carefully trekking over the debris on the forest floor, quickly depleted their energy. Supplies were distributed on the backs of those who could take the extra weight, including the children. There were babies to be carried and the elderly to help navigate the terrain. Clouds of black flies and mosquitoes attacked them all day long. They were always hungry, cold, infested with bites, dirty, and exhausted.

One of their stops was at Toussaint Blandchard's house. Here, Father Jean-Baptiste de la Brosse, the local missionary had set up a temporary chapel after the destruction of the Chipoudie and Petitcodiac churches in the fall of 1755. Mr. Blanchard's house, located on the west side of the Petitcodiac River, was on the direct path to Île Saint-Jean where many refugees took a well-deserved break on their journey. Children born just before or after the exodus, and marriages whose planned events had been disrupted by the war, were being baptized and blessed at the Blanchard house. As the large group of Comeaus came upon Toussiant Blanchard's house for a rest, Francois's nephew, Michel, and his sweetheart, Marie Madeleine, realized an opportunity to get married. They had planned the wedding before their sudden escape from the area. It was March 19th. Marie Madeleine was fourteen-years-old, and Michel was twenty-three.

After a short pause, they continued to brave the bitterly cold spring weather of 1756, cached in the woods. With snow still on the ground, signs of spring were barely noticeable. But the knowledge that the month of April was just around the corner gave them hope of reaching Île Saint-Jean before summer. When they finally reached Baie Verte on the coastline, Anne, Francois's wife, became very ill and was struggling to continue on the journey. She was not the only one. Many were suffering from malnutrition and exhaustion.

"We will stop here, eat, and rest properly," one of the men suggested. "It will take us a few days to build some canoes to get across the bay." They all agreed. They would rest on the banks, on piles of leaves, or wherever they could find a patch of moss. They had left with as many provisions as they could, but by now, very little remained. The evening meal, their only meal, consisted of whatever was available. A fire would be quickly lit and a pot of water put to boil. Often, a hot tea beverage made of the leaves and berries they picked along the way was their only nourishment for the day. If they were lucky enough to trap a rabbit or snag a fish, it did not provide enough food. There were too many mouths to feed and many went hungry.

The Acadians were well acquainted with the construction of birch bark canoes and proficient at building them. They had mastered this trade, learned from their ancestors who had been taught by the Mi'kmaq.

"Can you, your brother, and your cousins start peeling off bark from the trees?" Francois asked his fourteen-year-old son, also named Francois.

So young Francois gathered all the adolescent cousins together, those old enough to use a knife and went off into the bush.

Meanwhile, mothers and daughters began gathering as many spruce and pine roots as they could find, splitting them and placing them in a pot of boiling water to soften them. The men built canoe frames, made from rough-cut cedar, also soaked in water and then bent to the shape of the canoe. The young lads returned with large sheets of bark scraped from the birch trees.

"Well done," expressed the men when they surveyed the huge pile of bark the boys had scavenged. "It won't take us too long to get these canoes ready."

The group worked tirelessly, in unison, with one goal in mind. Finally, the canoes were ready to transport them from Baie Verte, across the Northumberland Strait, to Port Lajoie on Île Saint-Jean.

~~~~~~

Just like the spruce trees whose roots are connected beneath the forest floor, as if they are holding hands, supporting each other, so were the Acadians entwined. They gained their strength by standing together, side by side, arm in arm, hand in hand, forming an unbreakable bond. They encouraged one another and guided each other as they endured the horrendous events of the Great Upheaval.

When they finally arrived at Port Lajoie, Île Saint-Jean, the group suffered tremendous losses. The exhaustion and hunger from their journey were extremely demanding on the group, and many died. Among the dead were Francois's wife, Anne Lord and his nephew, Jean Comeau, Brigitte's first husband. Francois's brother-in-law, and his sister-in-law (Anne's sister) also passed away within a few weeks of making it to safety. No one could have predicted how the treacherous journey fleeing the English would have ended in such tragedy.

Brigitte was now widowed with six children. So shortly after their arrival, on August 26, 1756, Francois's eldest son, Maurice, married Brigitte in a small ceremony. They exchanged vows in the presence of Maurice's five younger siblings, his father, an uncle, and a nephew. Maurice vowed to protect her and her children, and support them financially.

"*Felicitation!*" Francois congratulated his son on his wedding day.

"Thanks," responded Maurice solemnly. "I wish Mother could have been present for this occasion. It's so difficult to celebrate and be joyous when we are still grieving her loss."

There were sniffles of grief amongst the children and sniffles of joy from others for the newly wedded couple. It was not an overly joyous occasion, but they were grateful for having arrived at what they perceived as a new home, a safe haven on French soil.

But Francois and the many Acadians who sought refuge on the island were disillusioned. Believing that Île

Saint-Jean would provide them with the same lifestyle and comfort they were accustomed to in Chipoudie, they were sorely mistaken. Little did they know that this would only be a temporary reprieve for most of them. The additional population put a burden on the small island's economy. Île Saint-Jean didn't have the resources to support them all. And those determined to stay and make it a permanent home would only endure more hardships when the British came to seize the island in 1758.

There was no land available, and food was scarce. To lighten the load, the colonial administrator of the island began to send several shiploads of Acadians to New France during the summer of 1756. One hundred and ninety-seven Acadians left Île Saint-Jean at the end of September 1756 and disembarked at the port of Quebec on October 18, 1756. Amongst the passengers selected for the voyage were the weakest, the elderly, the widows, the widowers, and orphaned children. With five dependent children, fifty-six-year-old Francois fit the requirements. Making the journey with him were Maurice and his new wife, Brigitte, and her children. It was perhaps a stroke of good luck or fate but this fortunate turn of events that led them to board a ship saved them from further hardship. There is no doubt that leaving Île Saint-Jean before the British took control was a godsend to this family and finally put an end to their transient lifestyle. By the end of 1756, approximately six-hundred Acadians were in New France. It was a bittersweet reunion for the Acadians who had survived. For Francois and his family, it was a chance to reconnect with daughter Marie Anne who had married Louis Rousse in Chipoudie and relocated to New France a year earlier.

While Maurice and his wife successfully escape the British deportation with his father Francois, and the rest of his siblings, Brigitte's eldest son, Victor, did not. Instead, he and his cousins Charles and Michel (who had newly-wed at Toussaint Blanchard's house earlier that spring) became separated from the group. Caught by the British in 1759, they were imprisoned on Georges Island in Halifax and held there until the end of the war. Eventually, they were sent to San Domingo in Haiti, but like most other deportees, they could not adapt to the extremely hot climate. After a traumatic journey of hiding in the woods, finding temporary refuge in Île Saint-Jean, escaping a second time, and eluding capture by hiding along the St. John River, then being captured and imprisoned in Halifax for five years, they finally arrived in Louisiana. It was February 1765, ten years after they left Chipoudie. Here, they found hope for starting a new and better life - amongst other fellow Acadians.

Nine months after the ships arrived in Quebec City from Île Saint-Jean, Fort Louisbourg on Île-Royale (Cape Breton Island) was seized by the British. Louisbourg had been the seat of government for both Île-Royale, and Île Saint-Jean. Over thirty-five hundred Acadians from these two islands were loaded onto sixteen ships and sent to France, across the stormy winter seas of the Atlantic Ocean. The voyages of these ships were longer and more dangerous than the ships sent to the British colonies in 1755. The conditions were extremely harsh for the passengers, especially the children. Many Comeaus were on these ships but by our good fortune, Francois had left Île Saint-Jean just in the nick of time.

Three ships, the Violet, the Duke William, and the Ruby, all sank in the North Atlantic Ocean. On the Ruby, seventy-seven passengers had died of disease before it hit rocks at Pico Island (Azores) and sank. Another one-hundred and thirteen, along with three crew members, died in the shipwreck. The Violet, carrying approximately two hundred and eighty Acadians, sank on December 12, 1758. Ninety passengers had previously perished on board from the appalling conditions.

The deadliest day of the deportations occurred on December 13, 1758, when the ship, the Duke William, carrying over three hundred and sixty passengers, encountered a fatal storm. Only four persons survived. It is considered one of the greatest marine disasters in Canadian history. Francois Raymond, Anne Comeau's son (Francois' nephew), was on this ship. When all the boats carrying the deported Acadians had arrived at their ports of destination in France, almost half had drowned or succumbed to illness.

After the British captured the two islands and raided the Gaspé and the Saint-John River, many Acadians, not yet captured, fled to St Pierre and Miquelon, an island still under France's rule, off the coast of Newfoundland. When the war ended in 1763, St Pierre and Miquelon became a place of refuge. Again, the Acadians believed they would be safe there and live in peace, but the small islands couldn't support them. Three years later, the government sent them to France because the colony became overpopulated. With France now supporting all of these exiles, it placed a significant burden on the country, and the following year France revoked its decision. Once again, most of these Acadians were deported back to Miquelon. More wars erupted between the French and the English, causing two more subsequent deportations in 1778 and 1794. Finally, when England relinquished control in 1815 deportees from France began returning to the island.

Throughout the deportation years, the Comeau families were deported throughout the British colonies: Maryland, Connecticut, Massachusetts, North Carolina, South Carolina, New York, Pennsylvania, Virginia, and Georgia. Some were exiled in England. Many were forced to flee to Saint-Pierre and Miquelon, PEI, Cape Breton, New Brunswick, Nova Scotia, and Quebec. And not by choice, some ended up in Louisiana, Haiti, Dominican Republic, Martinique, and Guadeloupe. Various attempts to settle Acadians in Corsica, the Falkland Islands, and French Guiana failed. In these regions, the settlers were subject to high mortality given the numerous tropical diseases and harsh climate.

~~~~~~

It appeared that no one cared for or had any compassion for the Acadians. They had been displaced, abandoned, and rejected all over the world, not once, not twice, but as many as five times. And for some families this lasted for a period of more than thirty years.

I often think about the circumstances of Francois and his children leaving Île Saint-Jean just a few short months before the island was seized and all the inhabitants were shipped to France where fifty percent of them perished along the way. If that had been our destiny, there would have been a good chance that our lineage would have ended abruptly. And even if they would have survived the journey, I would not be the one telling you this story. Instead, another Comeau descendant, would be telling you a much different story. Whatever you might call it: a fluke, a stroke of luck, a blessing, a good fortune, boarding that ship bound for Quebec was a godsend to Francois, his family and all of his descendants.

The stoicism of the Acadian families who endured so much hardship demonstrates their remarkable human will in the face of cruelty. Imagine travelling for several months through the winter, hiding in the woods, fearful of being captured by the soldiers, and losing your loved ones along the way! This would be an endurance test that only the most physically and psychologically fit persons could survive. Most could never overcome this tragic course of events, and like a debilitating disease, it would leave them crippled for life.

Chapter 12

Becancour, New France – 1757

In New France, the mortality rate of the Acadians soared once again. Numerous diseases such as yellow fever, scurvy and typhoid were common but not as devastating or rampant as smallpox, which killed more than five hundred Acadians between November 1757 to March 1758. *La petite verole* or *la picotte*, the French term for smallpox was recorded in the New France parish registers, along with the letters *acc* or *acad* in the margin, to identify Acadian heritage. Amongst the victims were twenty Comeaus: Francois's brothers, sisters, in-laws, nephews, and nieces who died at L'Hopital Hotel-Dieu-de-Quebec. On April 28, 1758, Francois succumbed to the disease; he was fifty-eight years old.

How sad to have endured a treacherous journey from Acadia to PEI and New France, only to die upon arriving.

Francois's four unmarried children were now orphans. Ranging in age from eleven years old to twenty-one, they still required someone to provide for them. Fortunately, their eldest sister Marie Anne and her husband, Louis Rousse, were already established in New France by the time the rest of the family arrived. Also in New France to help support them were their older brother, Maurice and his new bride, Brigitte.

The voyage had been stressful for Maurice and Brigitte. Brigitte's eldest son, Victor, and his two cousins had missed the sailing from Île Saint-Jean, but Brigitte hoped that someday they would find their way to New France and be reunited. Unfortunately, that would not be the case. They had joined the militia, led by Joseph Broussard. After years of fighting and turmoil, they were captured and imprisoned in Halifax. In prison, Victor had married Anne Michel, a fellow Acadian with a young child and were transported to Louisiana after the war, arriving in February 1765 with the Broussard party. Their son, Jean, was born in Haiti along the way. They never reunited with their families again.

Once again, the Acadians found that Quebec City would only be a temporary camp for them. They were housed in naval hangars located near the quay. Some were lodged with families who were paid for housing and feeding them. Francois Bigot, the Intendant of New France, and his myrmidons were thieves. The Acadians who managed to bring a little money and a few household treasures with them were robbed. They were only allowed four ounces of bread a day and forced to scrounge the gutters for food. During the winter of 1756-

1757, many died of starvation because of a food shortage. The New France hosts regarded them as burdens rather than allies in their struggle against the British. Soon after their arrival, the government anticipated an attack from the British and began to disperse the refugees to several different localities in New France.

The Seven Years' War was not over. In 1758, when the British seized Île Saint-Jean and the fortress of Louisbourg on Île-Royale (Cape Breton), it left New France exposed. The British could now sail undetected up the St. Lawrence River and overtake Quebec City. In 1759, at the Plains of Abraham, the British successfully captured Quebec City. Under British sovereignty, New France became known as the Province of Quebec. This event was a pivotal moment that changed the course of history for the French and Canada.

In 1763 by the Treaty of Paris, France lost all of its claims to the territories in mainland North America in exchange for some Caribbean Islands, and the promise to allow French Canadians to freely practice Catholicism, and the right to fish off the coast of Newfoundland. That's it? Unbelievable! France lost all of Acadia, all of New France, all of New Brunswick, all of Prince Edward Island and all of Cape Breton and eventually all of Canada for a few concessions and the islands of Martinique and Guadeloupe! They valued the profitable sugar trade over the vast Canadian lands because Canada had been a constant financial burden on them. What a débâcle! What an oversight! France had abandoned its people, not only on the battlefield but at the table with a quill and paper.

Francois and Anne's refuged children eventually found a permanent home in New France, settling in the Becancour region. Their son Francois who had left Chipoudie as a young thirteen-year-old boy was now twenty-five years old and married to Francoise Paris-La-Madeleine. They had three children. When Francoise passed away, he married Genevieve Dubois in 1774 and raised nine more children.

Comfortably settled with a family of his own, Francois began telling his children the stories of his ancestors and their origins in Acadia, first-hand accounts of the deportations, and the tragic events that brought them to Quebec. The children would gather around and beg their father for a story.

"Tell me a story, papa, about the olden days," asked Michel, Francois and Genevieve's youngest child. They crowded around him as he began narrating actual historical events, embellishing them just enough to keep their young minds interested and questioning. He had mastered the age-old craft of storytelling, taking the children on a new and exciting journey, no matter how many times they had heard the same story.

"What story would you like to hear tonight?" he asked, knowing that they would choose their favourite one.

So, Charles blurted out, "The Adventures of Antoine Comeau and Dorcus Wooden".

The three young children, Michel, four, Charles, eight, and Genevieve, ten, agreed. From their wide-eyed expressions, it would appear that Francois was about to spin straw into gold as he began the story:

"A long, long time ago, your great-great-great grandfather Pierre Comeau and his wife Rose Bayon were living in Acadia with their nine children. Their sixth child was named Antoine, and he married a lady named Dorcus Wooden. Although Antoine was an ordinary child, just like everyone else, he felt different. For example, while all the children his age would like to be out running and playing, Antoine preferred sitting under the big oak tree behind the Chapel, drawing circles with two sticks connected with a string. He had crudely constructed a compass, one that mimicked precisely what his father's compass did, draw circles.

Some neighbourhood children would ask, what is that, pointing to his homemade contraption. He always took the time to show them how it worked. At an early age, Antoine was engrossed in the scientific field of study encompassing mathematics, mechanics, and empirical research. The children his age did not understand his drawings, and everyone else thought his ideas were grandiose or foolish, except for Monsieur Louis Allain.

Louis had sailed to Wells, Maine, from France. He quickly became a prominent businessman in Maine, owning one hundred acres, a house, a mill, and a blacksmith shop. Later he came to Port Royal, acquiring more property and establishing a grain mill, a blacksmith shop, and a store. He travelled back and forth from Acadia to Maine on his ship named the Endeavor and spoke excellent English and French.

Louis was seven years older than Antoine, but he became his friend and mentor. Antoine often hung out at his blacksmith shop, working by his side, absorbing as much knowledge about the trade as he could. Louis liked the young man, and they often engaged in conversations regarding engineering, design, and business.

Antoine also liked going into the Chapel, not necessarily to pray; he enjoyed the solitude and the quietness. It was his favourite place to think, visualize and fantasize.

Antoine grew up to be a fine young man. While many people described him as a dreamer, his parents, Pierre and Rose, knew him to be caring, compassionate, and understanding. Over the years, they witnessed his calm demeanour, his kindness, and his desire to please everyone. Antoine surrendered to whatever his siblings wanted to avoid conflict and keep the peace. They thought that because young Antoine possessed such excellent qualities, he would be well-suited for the priesthood. So they began encouraging him to follow what they believed would be his calling.

When Antoine turned 23 years old, they paid for his passage aboard a ship bound for France, where he was to receive his seminary education. The year was 1684.

But Antoine had his own ideas. Ever since his parents had mentioned the priesthood, Antoine had been dreaming up alternate plans. He did not feel that the priesthood was his calling, or it was the vocation he desired. He had envisioned himself as an inventor, an engineer, or a builder. After seeing him embark on his ship destined for France, Pierre and Rose left the pier and never heard from Antoine again.

Antoine was secretly watching them, and once they were out of sight, he quickly got off the ship and bolted to

Louis's ship, the Endeavor. It was set to sail to Maine shortly, and Antoine was determined to be on board. The plan he had concocted in his head was much, much bigger than just abandoning France for Maine.

In Maine, Anthony Coombs worked as a forger. Anthony loved the work, creating objects from iron or steel by heating the metal and using tools to hammer, bend, and cut the hot metals into shapes. Anthony spent hours designing new instruments, agricultural implements, decorative and religious items, cooking utensils, and weapons. Anthony would begin heating pieces of steel until the metal became very soft. Using his hand tools, a hammer, and an anvil, he would pound the metal and shape it into various objects."

Francois goes on and on about the trade of blacksmithing, Anthony this and Anthony that, waiting for the children to get bored and restless.

"Oh, papa! Enough already", the children sighed. "We know it is Antoine!"

It had become a tradition since the first time he had told the story. The children had sat patiently listening to Francois go on and on about Anthony Coombs and the blacksmithing trade, and had finally blurted: "Who is Anthony Coombs?"

"Ah, yes it is Antoine, of course." Francois continues. "He had arranged to work as a blacksmith on contract in his friend Louis Allain's blacksmith shop. He had changed his name to Anthony Coombs. It was part of his plan. No one would ever know what happened to him. No one could ever find him. How brilliant was he? La fin!"

"Non, pas la fin!" Michel lamented.

"We want to hear about Dorcus Wooden," they all whined.

"Another night. You know it is a two-part story. Allons-y," came the peremptory reply from his father.

Of course, the children obeyed immediately, but not without the usual sighs, groans, and aahs!

Like most Acadians, Francois loved sharing these stories with his children. The tales told of Comeau's adventures during the deportations, the escapes, the imprisonments, the exiles, and the refugees in hiding, provided a historical account of their family's journey. The stories were not only entertaining, but they were also great examples for instilling moral values, and teaching work ethic and perseverance to the children.

Who wouldn't want to hear 'Mutiny on the Pembroke', a story about four of Anne Comeau's children who, with other passengers, conspired against the ship's crew and managed to overtake the Pembroke ship destined to take them to North Carolina? Or the 'Cat-O-Nine-Tails Whipping', the story of Francois, another child of Anne Comeau's, (it appears she may have had a few mischievous kids) who was sentenced to this severe and cruel method of punishment for his involvement in mischiefs and petty thefts. And 'Simon Says', about Simon Comeau and his family who endured at least five deportations, including being exiled in Britain for seven years, and finally settling in Louisiana? There were many stories about their ancestor's hardships and suffering. Each one had been transformed into a heart-warming account that was emotionally rewarding and uplifting.

Like his father before him, young Michel grew up and became a farmer. He continued the rich tradition of storytelling about the Acadians to his children and grandchildren. Michel married Marie Angele Parmentier in Becancour, where they settled. While most took the church's advice to heart: "to leave home and create a family as soon as the resources were available", Michel and Angele were both thirty years old on their wedding day. During the mid-1800s, life expectancy in Canada was only forty years, so the earlier a couple married the greater number of childbearing years could be expected. Michel and Angele had a late start but still managed to have seven children. The last one was born when they were both forty-six years old.

Four of Michel and Marie Angele's sons, Elzear, Alexis, Noel, and Felix, established families and continued the farming legacy on land just a couple of miles from Ste. Gertrude parish. This small community began to develop quickly in 1845, along with numerous other parishes in the Becancour region. The Comeau boys were fortunate to acquire rich fertile land which yielded abundant crops of wheat, potatoes, and turnips. A stream named *Ruisseau* Comeau flowed quietly through their properties, providing their operation with pure, clear water and a necessary watering hole for their animals. The area was also renowned for its quality of trees suitable for construction. The massive oaks, elms, beeches, maples, and pines on their property enabled them to build homes and barns to last a lifetime.

Almost overnight, the Ste. Gertrude's area had flourished. The Gertrudian population more than doubled in the first twenty years. The community built a road, five to six miles long, that connected the area of Ste. Gertrude to the Becancour River, which greatly contributed to the expansion of the area. Also, agriculture became very lucrative because it occupied a part of the basin of the Gentilly river. Here clays were deposited by the Champlain Sea, a sea that existed long ago and eventually shrunk and disappeared as the area began to rise above sea level. The logging industry for timber and firewood exploded, and maple syrup production became profitable. These activities led to the opening of various flour, wool, and lumber mill.

Before caring for the Ste. Gertrude church and grounds, it was here that Elzear and Celina had erected a house and started raising their large family.

Chapter 13

Harry

What had happened to Antoine Comeau? All traces of him had disappeared after the 1686 Acadia Census. All his other siblings had been accounted for, but he was missing. Speculation that he had returned to France had become the most plausible scenario, and while no proof existed, most Comeau genealogy books cited this as fact.

It was recently discovered through DNA testing that Antoine Comeau and Anthony Coombs are very likely to be the same person. It is believed that Antoine Comeau moved from Port Royal to Maine in 1684 and had a blacksmith apprenticeship contract with Louis Alain who anglicized his name to Lewis Allen. It seems fitting that Antoine would also anglicize his name to Anthony Coombs.

Genealogy is constantly changing. Each year more research is completed, more records are indexed and made available and more DNA is collected to verify lineage. It is now understood that genealogy must be authenticated with a document, a record or a verbal story passed down. If you don't have a reliable source, it is not fact.

Earlier I mentioned how some families chose to give two of their children the same name and how confusing that might be. But often even more confusing for genealogists was when an individual, at some point in their lives, chose a name different other than what their birth record indicated. For example, how did Elzear's wife become Celina, when she was baptized Marie Dina? Did she change her name because she didn't like it or did the priest make an error in recording it in the parish registry? Interestingly, the only document where Celina is named "Dina" other than her baptismal record is in the baptismal record of her fifth daughter, Eugenie: "baptised Marie Eugenie… of the legitimate marriage of Elzear Comeau and Dina Doucette.." And even more confusion is triggered when daughter Eugenie mysteriously becomes "Virginie" after the 1861 census. Did she choose to change her name on a whim? Why do all subsequent documents record her name as Virginie, including her wedding to Julian Richards, in all of her children's birth and her death record in the Little Falls Herald in 1917? It is not surprising that many genealogy sites document 'Eugenie' and 'Virginie' as being two separate, individual children of Elzear and Celina.

It never ceases to amaze me how many records were saved throughout all of the war years, the deportations, and even when churches were burned to the ground. When you're immersed in genealogy, there is no greater joy than to stumble upon a record, like a wedding document from 1756 that took place in the woods while the bridal party was fleeing from the British, or a census record from seventeenth century that describes a family, each of their children and their ages, their servants, and all of their possessions and acquisitions. In this story there are very few instances where the dates for births, marriages, deaths and events were not authenticated by a record.

Chapter 14

Gertrude, Quebec - 1870

In late August, Elzear married my great-grandmother, Francoise Leblanc. She was a thirty-seven-year-old spinster, redheaded with light-coloured eyes and pale skin that would burn easily in the sun. She was a warm and caring person, shy, and sensitive, with a mild temperament. She would be a good match for Elzear. Surprisingly though, knowing how prolific the Leblanc family was in Acadia, I would have imagined that she was an Acadian. But not so. Her ancestors, also from France, had immigrated directly to New France in the early 1600s.

The wedding preparations had been in the planning stages by Elzear's daughters for quite some time. They were excited about their father's nuptials, especially Melanie. At sixteen years old, Melanie was courting Joseph Bourque, and their relationship had blossomed quickly. The two had been careful not to display affection openly around the family. No one suspected that love was in the air.

"Which dress will you wear for the wedding, Francoise?" Melanie suddenly blurted when the girls were sitting together with Francoise. "What about the pale blue dress? It is so lovely with your *cheveux roux*," she added. "Will you add some lace to the dress?"

Her sudden giddiness and excitement for her father's wedding should have given her away. She was love-struck.

"Oh, I am not sure yet. Either the beige one or the light blue dress will be fine," Francoise replied, unconcerned. "Now, let me help with the supper," intentionally shifting the wedding attire conversation elsewhere. They were having a simple meal of pork pies with turnips and carrots. Francoise had come over earlier to make the pies. The girls already knew how to make *tourtieres*. This get-together was meant to be an afternoon of camaraderie with their future stepmother.

Two weekly publications, *Le Messenger de Nicolet* and *Le Journal d'Arthabaska* provided the community and surrounding area with news of upcoming events, the Bishop's visits, and church affairs. However, announcements for baptisms, weddings, and funerals were read to the congregation at church or communicated by word of mouth including the banns, and dates of an impending marriage. Newborn children were baptized as soon as possible, usually the same day or the next day. These events could easily pack a church if they occurred when the weather was agreeable for travel, and it was not during harvest season. It was open for anyone to attend and did not require an invitation. No one ever knew how many people would attend. It was always a surprise.

On the wedding day the two oldest girls, Agnes and Melanie, woke up at the crack of dawn and bolted to the church grounds to cut flowers. It was the end of August and most of the blooms were already spent. Luckily, they found some volunteer wildflowers, haphazardly growing where they had re-seeded themselves. The girls gathered bundles of wild bergamot with clusters of purple flowers that looked like ragged pompoms and combined them with stems of yarrow and black-eyed-susans. The fernlike lacy stems and the creamy flower heads of the yarrow created a good filler. They made two bouquets and tied each with a strip of calico fabric, beige with little blue cornflowers, ripped from an old blouse destined for the rag bin. Melanie carefully placed these near the alter while Agnes picked a few more stems to take home for the bride. The wedding at Ste. Gertrude's church was simple, small, and intimate. The children and a few family members were the only guests in attendance.

The entry in the parish registry translates as follows:

'The twenty ninth of August, eighteen hundred and seventy, after the publication of two bans of marriage in our parish according to the very reverend Ch. Ol. Caron, V.G., dated the twenty sixth current month between Elzear Comeau, living in this parish, of majority age, widower of Celina Doucet, in part; and Francoise Leblanc, also from this parish, daughter of majority age, of Francois Xavier Leblanc and deceased Victoire Champoux, in part, without any present impediment, we, undersigned, priest of Ste. Gertrude have received their mutual consent to marriage and have given them the nuptial blessing in the presence of Felix Comeau, the groom's brother, Francois Xavier Leblanc, the bride's father, Antoine Leblanc, the bride's uncle, Joseph Hamel, bride's brother in law and a large number of other persons, a few who have signed with the groom, the bride declared that she did not know how to sign.'[5]

It was a sunny Monday, and as it was customary in those days, the wedding was at ten o'clock in the morning. Everybody was back to their daily routine by noon.

Immediately Francoise fit into this well-established family and eased into the daily routine without stepping on any toes. The older girls accustomed, to a routine, each with their assigned duties, continued to keep the house tidy, tend to the garden, and cook.

When Celina passed away, her three youngest boys, Phileas, Onesiphore, and Omer were 6, 5 and 3 respectively. It was Francoise who nurtured and raised these boys together with her own children. At this time little did Elzear know that he would have another four children, including my grandfather Arthur. Francoise, became pregnant almost immediately after their wedding and gave birth to: Albert, Arsene, Arthur, and daughter, Rosana. Unfortunately, Arsene passed away before his third birthday. Arthur and his half-siblings Phileas, Onesiphore and Omer grew up together, never for a minute considering each other to be half-siblings. They were always 'brothers'.

In the fall, there was a second wedding. Melanie and Joseph exchanged vows on October 10th and settled in the same parish on the Bourque land with his mother, Leocadie. Joseph had been farming the land since his father passed away. The Bourque family were also some of the original settlers in Acadia in the mid-1600s, whose name was then known as Bourg. It seemed that everyone was related.

Chapter 15

Harry

Over several generations in our lineage, numerous ties were forged between the Comeau families and Acadian families. The Acadian families of Doucet, Bourg, Lord, Savoie, and Thibodeau to name a few, appear multiple times across multiple generations. It was common for siblings from one family to marry siblings from another family, which strengthened the community's blood ties. Often, brothers, sisters, aunts, and uncles chose life partners from the same lineage as another family member. This group of early Acadians became meshed over the next ten generations and beyond. You could say that they were not only connected downward like roots but also horizontally, like rhizomes. Below the ground, we were tied together, linked and intertwined every which way, like roots and rhizomes.

Sometimes I think I may be my own fifth cousin six times removed and that our family tree doesn't resemble a tree at all, but looks more like a wild bush of the Saskatchewan prairie.

Chapter 16

Ste. Gertrude, Quebec – 1879

Elzear was fifty-one years old when my grandfather, Arthur was born. So it was his older half-brothers who provided all the attention the younger ones needed. Phileas had been delegated the task of storytelling and he did this with such enthusiasm, and lots of theatrics. He always kept the children entertained. Tonight he would be telling the story about their distant cousins' courage and bravery aboard the ship, the Pembroke. They had defied all odds of escaping deportation and as far as historians know, they were the only Acadians to do so successfully.

So the children gathered around and listened attentively as Phileas got into character. By covering one eye with his hand to mimic an eye patch, making a fist with the other and pointing his curved index finger downward, he began to hobble about pretending he had a peg leg. All he needed now was a sword and a parrot to complete the pirate look and tell the tale of 'Mutiny on the Pembroke'.

"Argh! Mutiny on the Pembroke might conjure images of pirates like the one-eyed, hook-handed, peg-legged robbers who plundered the ships of the seas in search of treasure. Argh!" Phileas began.

The children burst into fits of giggles! My great-grandmother, Francoise, called out, "Phil, you are getting the children all riled up, it's bedtime, quiet time, not playtime." Immediately Phileas returned his contorted body to his natural position, the children settled down and he continued the story:

"This legendary tale is about a mutiny on the Pembroke ship and the determination of the Acadian passengers. It's not about evil pirates pilfering for treasure.

Christmas was just around the corner. But even though they were preparing for the glorious occasion of the birth of Christ, it was not a joyous time for the Acadians. They were in the middle of the greatest upheaval in their lives. Across from the town of Port Royal, at Goat's Island, the Acadians observed a ship that had arrived and dropped anchor. The proudly displayed flag on the vessel did not bear any Fleurs-de-Lis! They sensed trouble!

Sure enough! Within a few hours, the British appeared to round up the Acadians for deportation. They were ordered to move along by a crew member. One by one, the Acadians were forced, pushed and crammed down below in the cargo hold of the ship with the animals, food, and supplies. No explanation was given, but the Acadians knew what was happening! The British were in the process of gathering all the Acadians in the land and deporting them to the British Colonies. Why? Because the British wanted the land in Acadia for themselves - for their British people.

Their ship, the Pembroke, was a Snow, a two-masted vessel with a capacity of 139 tons. Captain Milton was at the helm of the ship. He ordered two-hundred and thirty-two Acadians onto the ship. Amongst the group were four of Anne Comeau and Francois Raymond's adult children and their families. Jean-Baptiste, Charles, Joseph, and sister, Anne, were living quite happily in Port Royal with their families until that day. Their father, Francois Raymond, had been a soldier of the fort in Port Royal and he had married Anne Comeau, your great-great-grand Aunt. All together on the Pembroke were twenty Raymond children and an additional eighteen other cousins whose mothers were Comeaus married into the Guilbeau, Melanson, and Petitot-dit-Saint-Seine families.

What an adventure for these children!

Where are we going? they asked. No one answered them.

The captain and his crew smirked as they pulled up anchor and snickered 'bon voyage' to all. The captain did not disclose their destination. It was 5 o'clock in the morning on December 8, 1755, and they were going to North Carolina.

Just outside of the Bay of Fundy, they joined a fleet of six vessels led by a frigate to guide their way. Their living conditions below were far from ideal, but they managed to keep a positive outlook on their situation. Among them were many friends and relatives. They knew everyone.

Un, deux, trois, quatre, counted Felicite Guilbeau, standing against a wooden post, keeping her hands tightly over her eyes. At times, there would be fifty children engaged in a game of hide and seek. When the counting started, the sheer number of children running about resembled an infestation of mice scrambling at the sight of a big cat. It created a noisy, confusing disturbance but kept the children occupied. The crew had given strict orders and warned them to keep themselves and the children quiet at all times. That was IMPOSSIBLE!

While the children kept busy with games, the adults waited patiently for their turn up on deck. With an allotment of twenty minutes each, only six people were allowed at a time to climb through the hatch and get fresh air.

Somewhere near St. Mary's Bay, a violent storm ensued. A bank of blue-gray clouds appeared in the distance, and the temperature began to drop. Suddenly the sea turned completely white, and huge waves and hurricane-force winds battered the vessels. It pushed the Pembroke ship into St. Mary's Bay, separating it from the fleet.

Charles Belliveau believed that this was their opportunity for a coup and quickly devised a plan. He had noticed that there were only eight crew members and he knew that the group of Acadians could easily overtake them. This was possibly their only chance to escape. So when the next group were allowed to go up for air, six of the strongest men were sent up. When one of the crew members gave them the order to return below deck, Monsieur Beaulieu knocked a crew member down. He gave him a knuckle sandwich! It had all been preplanned. That was the signal to open the hatch and let all the men out! They came out charging at the crew. In just a few minutes, they had taken control of the ship. It was a daring exploit and a glorious victory!

Amongst the passengers were several Acadian captains who took turns at the helm. Now safe in the French waters of St. Mary's Bay, they were in no rush to leave. The ship had been adequately victualed; there was abundant food and drink, enough for 39 days. So they celebrated Christmas, had a few victory parties, and made plans to sail to the mouth of the St. John River.

Once they were anchored along the shore of the St. John River they rejoiced, and cheered. It was February 8th, two months after they had left Acadia. They were not on the land where they had established their homesteads, but they were in Acadia, on Acadian soil.

They were not pirates at all, but heroes indeed! They were the only Acadians, loaded on a ship, on their way to be deported, who escaped successfully. The end."

My grandfather loved the stories told by his brother, Phileas. These were pleasant times for the younger children with so many older half-siblings tending to their every need. Elzear and Francoise were still managing a full house with seven children: Leah, twenty-three, Phileas, Onesiphore, and Omer, teenagers, and the three younger half-siblings, Albert, nine, Arthur, six, and

Rosana, four. Agnes, Melanie, and Virginie were married and creating their own families. Also living with them for many years was my great-great-grandfather, Michel. He passed away just after Arthur was born.

Chapter 17

Harry

The Acadians had a reputation for being great raconteurs. Because of this, their stories were told and re-told over many generations and survived for their descendants to enjoy and cherish. While storytelling was in the Comeau blood it was never in my wheelhouse. I was always very modest, quiet, and reticent. I never felt the need to vocalize my achievements, successes, or failures. I never talked about my ancestors until now. I realize that storytelling is an important opportunity to share my values and beliefs and preserve my family's legacy. From the stories passed down generations ago, and the shared Acadian stories online from historians, genealogists and fellow Acadians, I was able to uncover the missing records to complete the gaps in the Comeau timeline. Now I am able to tell you the complete story about our journey from

France to Acadia to Quebec to Minnesota to Saskatchewan.

A couple of my favourite stories are about Joseph Broussard, and Jacques Rousse.

Joseph Broussard also known as Beausoleil, and his family were settlers in Chipoudie at the time of the deportation orders, so they were well-known within the community and by the Comeaus. Along with his sons, Joseph organized a Mi'kmaq and Acadian militia to fight against the British throughout the wars. It was with this group that many of Francois's nephews and relatives stayed behind to fight while the family escaped to Quebec. Joseph Broussard was revered as an Acadian hero, for bravely fighting and leading the Acadians to Louisiana to start a new life.

Jacques 'Jack, James' Rousse a.k.a. Rouse or Rowse, was the second son of Marie Anne Comeau and Louis Rousse. Jacques was born just a couple of years before the great upheaval, around 1753. He fought against the British in the American Revolution in 1775. When the Americans invaded Quebec, they had expected the French Canadians to pick up arms against the British and fight alongside them. But they had badly misjudged Canadian sentiment and most inhabitants remained stubbornly neutral – refusing to take up arms against either their British rulers or the American rebels.

But to some, the events of the Great Upheaval were still fresh in their minds and still left a bad taste in their mouths. The British remained their enemy for a long, long time, and the future generations, who were not as stubborn as the previous ones, sided with the Americans. Recalling the Acadian Deportation and how many young Acadian children were taken from their parents and indentured by the British, the presence of Acadian names among American soldiers is not surprising. But it is very ironic that our deported ancestors, whose many children were born along the eastern coast of the British colonies, would come back and engage in a battle for freedom for those colonies that were at times so cruel to them.

When the Americans battled to overtake Quebec from the English and failed, the American army was forced to retreat to New York. This led to a counter-invasion southward via Lake Champlain into New York, where the Americans fought and defeated the British. It was the first great American victory of the American Revolution. After the Revolution, Jacques Rousse settled here on the western shore of Lake Champlain, New York and Rouse's Point is named after him.

And did you know about *les Filles a Marier* and *les Filles du Roi*? During two separate periods in the mid to late 1600s, women from France left their homes to find a new life in the new world. Between 1634 and 1663, two hundred and sixty-two marriageable girls, *les Filles a Marier*, immigrated to New France. Most came alone, were between the ages of twelve and forty-five years old, and believed that the colony would offer them a better life. They are the true pioneers of New France. Afterwards, from 1663 to 1673, King Louis XIV sponsored approximately eight hundred women from

France, the King's Daughters, *les Filles du Roi*. Single French women were recruited and transportation to New France, paid for by the King. Their purpose was to marry the single male colonists and help populate the colony.

Although my ancestors were Acadians and none of the King's Daughters or Marriageable Girls landed in Acadia, we descend from many of these brave women through the maternal side of my great grandmothers, Genevieve Dubois, Angele Parmentier, and Francoise Leblanc who married my great grandfathers, Francois, Michel and Elzear.

They were:

Marie Jeanne Toussaint arrived in New France on July 31st, 1670 aboard the ship La Nouvelle France. (Genevieve Dubois - maternal side);

Catherine Veillot's aboard the ship, Le Louis de Dieppe, landed in New France on September 25th, 1667. (Genevieve Dubois - paternal side);

Renee Birette arrived in New France on July 30th, 1671, on the ship Le Prince-Maurice. (Angele Parmentier - maternal side);

Marie Robineau, sailed aboard La Nouvelle France, arriving on July 3rd, 1668. (Francoise Leblanc - paternal side).

What about Samuel de Champlain who left my grandmother Delphine's 6th great grandmother a good sum of money? Her name was Hélène des Portes and she was believed to be the first surviving child born to European parents in New France. She was goddaughter to Hélène Boullé, Champlain's wife and was among the beneficiaries of Champlain's will in 1635. It stated: 'I give three hundred pounds to Helene des Portes, my wife's godchild'. It would have been worth about five hundred dollars.

How are we related to Rene Leblanc, the notary who was immortalized in Henry Wadsworth Longfellow's poem Evangeline you may ask?. He was married to Marguerite Thebeau, the daughter of Jeanne Comeau, who was Francois's sister. Together Marguerite and Rene had seventeen children, including triplets and three sets of twins!

Here is an excerpt from Henry Wadsworth Longfellow's 'Evangeline':

'René Leblanc will be here anon, with his papers and ink-horn.
Shall we not then be glad, and rejoice in the joy of our children?'
As apart by the window she stood, with her hand in her lover's,
Blushing Evangeline heard the words that her father had spoken,
And, as they died on his lips, the worthy notary entered.
...
Bent like a labouring oar, that toils in the surf of the ocean,
Bent, but not broken, by age was the form of the notary public;
Shocks of yellow hair, like the silken floss of the maize, hung
Over his shoulders; his forehead was high; and glasses with horn bows
Sat astride on his nose, with a look of wisdom supernal.
Father of twenty children was he, and more than a hundred
Children's children rode on his knee, and heard his great watch tick.
Four long years in the time of the war had he languished a captive,
Suffering much in an old French fort as the friend of the English.
Now, though warier grown, without all guile or suspicion,
Ripe in wisdom was he, but patient, and simple, and childlike.
He was beloved by all, and most of all by the children;
For he told them tales of the Loup-garou in the forest,
And of the goblin that came in the night to water the horses,
And of the white Létiche, the ghost of a child who unchristened
Died, and was doomed to haunt unseen the chambers of children;

And how on Christmas even the oxen talked in the stable,
And how the fever was cured by a spider shut up in a nutshell,
And of the marvellous powers of four-leaved clover and horseshoes,
With whatsoever else was writ in the lore of the village.'[6]

Although perhaps not as epic or poetically composed as the story of Evangeline told by Longfellow, there are many, many more amazing stories that exist and are being retold in other Comeau and Acadian households throughout the world today. Our roots run deep on North American soil and we share ancestral grandparents with many prominent people in Canada, including Grace Elliot. When your ancestors are amongst some of the first European inhabitants in North America, pre-confederation, you have a lot of history and a lot of good stories.

Chapter 18

Ste. Gertrude, Quebec - 1884

One early January morning while Elzear was working inside the church, he noticed smoke billowing between the floorboards. "Fire! Fire!" Elzear screamed as he ran to sound the alarm. Before long, all the townspeople had gathered at the Church and were hauling buckets of water. Working in unison, they quickly doused the floor and extinguished the fire. It had been caused by a hot pipe. The floor had been severely burned, but thankfully the fire had been contained to a small portion of the church. Only smoke damage and burn marks could be found along one wall and the adjoining roof section. Repairs would cost about $150 - $200.

There were always minor repairs to accomplish around the church: a door that would no longer close because the frame had shifted, a latch that no longer engaged, and lots of painting to boot! But today, he had to repair the burnt-out portion of the floor and clean up the walls before mass could be celebrated on Sunday. Fixing the roof would have to wait. The Church needed a new roof long before the fire broke out, and Father Paul de Villers had decided to replace it with galvanized metal sheeting. Elzear knew of only one person to get this job done. When the weather was milder, he would hire Joseph Leblanc.

"Are you installing the new roof today?" Elzear waved to Joseph as he saw him coming up the road with his tools.

Joseph and Elzear were close friends, both good carpenters, but Joseph's skills extended far beyond carpentry. He was a roofer and had become somewhat of an expert in his trade - his work was highly praised by his customers. Because of this, he was in high demand, so Elzear was delighted to engage him for the job.

"Yes, you will have a new roof on the Church and Sacristy before long," Joseph yelled back.

It was the beginning of May and an opportune time to install a new metal roof. Not only would the leaks and the damage done by the fire be fixed, but the Church's appearance would also be enhanced.

It had been announced at church that visits from Bishop Mgr. Lafleche, to the Becancour area, would start the Sunday after Ascension. The Ste. Gertrude Parish would welcome him on May 30-31. A pastoral visit from the Bishop was a big to-do and it compelled the entire community to join in the renovations and the clean-up.

There was a shed to be built and repairs to the presbytery and the cleaning of the tithe barn. The tithe barn was used to store the parishioners' tithes paid in-kind, which was usually a tenth of a farm's annual harvest or earnings. It housed the animals, the feed, and the produce.

~~~~~~

Helping others and volunteering was in my nature, part of my DNA. If someone needed a hand, I would be there at the drop of a hat! Whether it was a neighbour needing a hand fixing a broken piece of machinery, a stranded motorist on the side of the road, or just one of my children in need of a simple oil change, I never hesitated. I believe that giving of yourself is one of the truly great secrets to being happy! Helping others just feels good.

The Bishop's objective was to: look at the parish community, ensure that religious education was provided for all ages, examine the financial state of the parish, and examine the record keeping. The Bishop would also come to celebrate the Eucharist, preach, and preside at confirmation. Albert, Arthur, Rosana, and the other eligible parish children were busy preparing for their confirmation.

After the roof was completed, the remaining days in May were dedicated to washing the pews, floors, walls, and windows, polishing the candelabras, and chalices, to ensure that everything was immaculate, just like the Holy man himself. Outside the church, trees and bushes were trimmed, flowers were planted, pathways swept, and the trim around the doors and windows repainted. It was a community effort. Everyone pitched in to complete the tasks. Everything had to be spic and span!

At home, Francoise prepared to host dinner for the two evenings the Bishop would be visiting. It would be a large gathering of relatives, neighbours, and friends. Like previous visits, which occurred every two to three years, Francoise and Elzear were gracious hosts, and the Bishop always left the parish well-fed and watered.

Elzear continued to care for the parish of Ste. Gertrude into his late fifties and dug the graves for many more family and friends: his father, his eldest daughter, Agnes, numerous grandchildren, and Father Paul De Villers, his closest friend.

Father De Villers provided spiritual guidance to the community of fifteen hundred Catholics for thirty years. Raised in a fairly wealthy family, Father had drawn upon his personal resources to help support the parish and parishioners. Under his administration, the church's exterior had been completed, and the interior had been richly decorated. He personally and generously took care of the purchase of ornaments, and the construction of the alters, pews, and vaults. He commissioned and donated nine paintings for the church, which were the work of a nun of the Sisters of the Good Shepherd of Quebec.

His dedication to the parish of Ste. Gertrude was evident. Father De Villers initiated many changes in the parish at his own expense, including the recent metal roof replacement on the Church and Sacristy. He built an Academy to instruct young girls from the parish and surrounding areas. Upon his death, he bequeathed this organization to the Sisters of Assumption with a good scholarship for its operation. It is not surprising that when the Ste. Gertrude parish was formally established as a village in 1901, it was named Villers in memory of him. He had been adored and highly respected by the parishioners. Elzear revered this man and felt his absence immensely.

Shortly after Father's passing, Elzear retired from his position as the church sexton. Elzear died on February 1, 1887, at the age of sixty-three. He was survived by his wife, Francoise of seventeen years, and nine of the fourteen children he bore.

As time passed on making a decent living became more and more difficult for young adults starting out in Quebec. In the late 1800s, newly married couples who were beginning to establish themselves and start families struggled to obtain farmland. Jobs were scarce. They leaned on their church and community for support when times were tough. Yet as difficult as it was for them to make a decent living, families always managed to donate generously to their church and support all the community's fundraising activities. There were raffles, bake sales, and concerts organized throughout the year to further raise money for the community.

"*Regard, regard,*" exclaimed Omer. "Read it for yourself. Our cousins will be playing in Warwick and Arthabaskerville next month! Let's plan to go!"

"*Oui! Ce groupe est si talentueux*! Allons-y!" Phileas chimed in.

An event, advertised in *Le Messenger de Nicolet* paper, had caught everyone's attention, especially the Comeaus. Two neighbouring towns were hosting a night of classical music performed by a sextet of musicians from Massachusetts and Connecticut. How exciting! Not only were the members of this group extremely talented, but they were also closely related! Six Comeau brothers, performing together, were one of the area's most beloved musical ensembles and recognized entertainers.

The brothers hailed from a very large family born in the parish of Saint-Medard-de-Warwick and had immigrated to the United States in the early 1880s. Due to bad weather, the original concert dates had been cancelled and new dates rescheduled. They would be playing thirty miles away in Arthabaskaville (renamed Victoriaville) at L.O. Pepin Hall on January 27 and in their hometown on February 3 at the Convent Hall. It was inevitable that both venues would fill up quickly, so the Comeau families, along with their Doucet and Leblanc cousins, made travel arrangements immediately.

The group did not disappoint. Each brother captivated the audience with their respective instruments. They played a melange of classical music, and familiar melodies of French-Canadian songs. It had been an unforgettable evening. All proceeds were donated to the local parishes!

But a few nights of fun weren't enough to keep the young adult Comeaus in Quebec. One by one, they began to migrate to the United States where they believed better employment opportunities existed. Quebec newspapers had been advertising good-paying lumber jobs in Minnesota, Wisconsin, and Louisiana for a long time, and this enticed many Quebecers to move.

Unemployment was high in the Becancour region. It was challenging to maintain a good living.

Omer left Quebec to find work in Minnesota in the mid-1880s. Not long afterwards, his brothers Phileas and Onesiphore followed suit. Their mother, Celina Doucet, had numerous siblings and cousins who had immigrated to the Little Falls area in the early 1870s and had become very well-established. With numerous Doucet cousins already living in Minnesota, the Comeau brothers would not be alone. Family would be there to welcome them and ease them into a new life, in a new country.

The journey from Quebec to Minnesota was not easy. Phileas, his wife, Marie and their two small children, boarded the train in Trois-Rivieres on an early April morning. They travelled an entire day through Montreal and onto Sarnia, with their heads leaning on the window, watching the Quebec landscape blur past them. Once in Sarnia, they crossed the St. Clair River by ferry and landed at the US Port of Entry, Port Huron. Relieved to have successfully met the entry requirements, they journeyed to Detroit, changed train lines and headed further west to Grand Haven, a small town, bordering Lake Michigan. A steamer awaited to carry them across Lake Michigan into Milwaukee. Another train brought them through Minneapolis and into Little Falls, Minnesota. They were ecstatic to hear the final train whistle blow, the conductor announcing Little Falls and the train wheels screeching to a halt. As they stepped out onto the platform, a cloud of steam from the engine billowed. When it cleared they found themselves in a new country, a different world.

It was an arduous journey that would not be repeated often, especially with small children. The stories of the deadly storms that sank steamers and caused collisions and fires between schooners, and the mysterious disappearances of many vessels were always circulating and weighing heavily on the traveller's minds. There were few choice routes for travellers; this was the most well-travelled and most convenient route.

With their siblings leaving Quebec one by one, and their father gone, brothers Albert and Arthur felt deserted. In 1889, they also left for Minnesota to begin a new life. Arthur was fifteen-years-old. Sister Virginie and her husband Julien joined them the following year. They all settled in Little Falls, Minnesota. Within just a few short years, six Comeau siblings had left Quebec. Their mother, Francoise, had almost been completely abandoned; only thirteen-year-old Rosana remained with her in Quebec.

Chapter 19

Little Falls, Minnesota – 1889

The crowd yelled "Surprise!" as Arthur walked into Felix's house. The going away party had been planned shortly after Arthur's arrival back in Little Falls. He was living with his brother Omer and had just found work in the lumber camps down in Louisiana. Felix and Mary's little house at 512 Second Street East was jam-packed with friends and relatives.

"Bring in more jugs from the back shed" Felix called out to Arthur, who was with a large group of men outside near the shed. It's where many of the men preferred to 'hang out'; where the booze was abundant and convenient and where they could talk "shop" in a manner that might possibly offend the ladies inside. It's where they preferred to party, where the large jugs of *piquette* and wine were stored.

"*Certainement*," replied Arthur, as he grabbed a couple of jugs of *piquette* and wine and made his way to the house.

"*Merci*, It's your last night in Little Falls, so let's make it a night to remember.

"*Oui, c'est du fun*. We're all having a great time! Thanks for having us all over."

The music of the fiddles, and the racket of the pots and spoons created a loud clangour, like a tintamare. The quick toe tapping and rapid jigging had everyone's glass of liquor sloshing over the edge. It was a lively party and Arthur loved a party. Life in the railway camps had introduced Arthur to alcohol very early on in his life and after having lived there for a long time, he'd acquired a taste for it.

~~~~~~

A young man, twenty-four years of age, enjoying a few drinks is not uncommon. But my experience with alcohol came at a much younger age. One of my earliest memories of alcohol was when I was in grade school. I usually came home with my lunch untouched; my appetite as a child was extremely poor, and my mother was very concerned. To remedy this, she would pack a small bottle of wine in my lunch pail. I'm not sure if this stimulated my appetite, but from early on, I acquired a taste for wine.

Like my grandfather, pouring drinks at social gatherings was my way of making guests feel comfortable, warm, and welcomed. It was a social lubricant to help put people at ease and lift their moods. It became part of my persona. I made homebrew, I made wine. My bar was always fully stocked in anticipation of company. I liked to pour a good stiff drink, and I was affectionately referred to as Harry Heavy Hand. I enjoyed the camaraderie, the friendship, and the socializing. I will always cherish the wonderful memories we created with our friends and family at the parties we hosted throughout our lifetime. Cheers! Salud! A Votre Sante!

In Little Falls, the Comeau boys were now known as Felix Como (Phileas Comeau), Oney Como (Onesiphore Comeau), Omer Como, and Arthur Como. The anglicized version of their names was better suited for the English environment of Little Falls. Since their arrival in Minnesota the brothers had been engaged at various employment. Arthur and his brother Albert immediately began working for the railway. This was Arthur's first experience in the workforce. He was young enough to adapt, strong enough to endure the physical labour and was able to persist in this field of work for a few years. Albert returned to Quebec in 1899 and moved to Nashua, New Hampshire, with his sweetheart, Marie Bergeron. They were married by Father Milette of St. Aloysius Church on October 17, 1899.

The day after the surprise party, a Tuesday afternoon, Arthur Como and a group of about thirty men, some still suffering from the effects of imbibing too much alcohol and lacking sleep from the night prior, left for Louisiana. The men would be employed by the Lecompte Lumber Company under the charge of M. Murphy, and work predominately on the Red River of the South.

Many of the northern lumbermen were moving into Louisiana, where the industry was just starting to flourish. It was the traditional: "to cut out and get out", the practice of moving or abandoning their mills after the local timber was cut. Louisiana was next to feel the lumberman's saw.

Little did Arthur know how rigorous the outdoor life of the loggers and rivermen would be when he started working. The winters were spent in primitive, bleak camps, isolated from populated areas. The bunkhouse facilities were damp, dirty, and cold, conditions that could not be easily tolerated by the meek and mild. Laundry was a task performed by the men themselves, outdoors using water heated on a campfire. Meals were eaten in the woods, prepared in the cooking shacks, and hauled out to the men on sleighs.

Once Arthur had gained logging experience, he returned to Minnesota the following winter to work for the Commonwealth Lumber Company in Frazee. This camp was closer to his home in Little Falls, where Arthur could hang out with his brothers and friends on his time off.

The lumber industry began to thrive in Minnesota in the late 1800s. Lumber companies had unlimited forests, enabling them to manufacture an abundance of milled products. Still, there were very few skilled men who were capable of swinging an axe and operating a saw available for hire. The many advertisements in the newspapers and trade journals failed to attract a sufficient number of workers; competition for manpower was fierce amongst mining companies, railroads, highway builders, and other public works projects.

Each sector required many workers, and new companies often struggled to retain a workforce needed for continuous production. The lumberjack lifestyle was not for everyone. Acres of trees were felled by hand, hauled by horses, and floated downstream to mills. It was challenging work that many could not endure, especially those who were not hardy or adventurous. Much of the work was seasonal, and employee turnover was extremely high.

The Little Falls population in 1890 was just under six thousand. There were seventeen saloons, numerous billiards halls, and restaurants patronized by large numbers of loggers and other seasonal workers in the town. Logging work was intense, with extended hours, harsh physical demands, and frequent danger. As a result, many did not stick around for long. This transient lifestyle developed the town's reputation for being rough and lively and created a colourful culture full of boozers and brawlers during these early years.

Drinking became a matter of great concern, not only in their town but in many parts of the state. An Anti-Saloon League had formed in 1898, a leading organization lobbying for prohibition in the USA. Anti-saloon League meetings were held regularly at the Little Falls Courthouse. Guest speakers who opposed the saloons claimed that they were the destroyers of the home, the ruin of the boys and girls growing to manhood and womanhood. They said saloons caused a large portion of insanity and crimes committed and the deterioration of the people. The advertisements for the meetings read: If you want to know what is causing the saloon people so much trouble and anxiety in the state of Minnesota, don't fail to be present at this meeting...

The Anti-Saloon League sent agents to monitor saloon activity and serve warrants to those not keeping the lid on. There were bitter wars between the town saloons and anti-saloon groups. While ordinances were in effect, many robberies and murders occurred as the population clashed over the drinking regulations. Towns voted whether they wanted to be wet towns or dry towns. Results would be published: the wets won by 20 votes or dry wins in another township! Before long, 1200 of the 1800 townships in Minnesota had no saloons.

Little Falls was no exception to the struggles between saloon owners, brewing companies, and the general public, especially those against dispensing intoxicating liquors. Kiewel Brewing Company had been established in Little Falls since 1893 and occupied a whole city block in the extreme northeast part of the city. Many wanted it closed up.

Before 1900 rolled around, the four Como men had pledged allegiance to the United States of America and became bona fide US citizens with fundamental rights and guaranteed protection by the Constitution. The process had been straightforward. As residents of Minnesota for the prerequisite time required, they were automatically granted citizenship by naturalization. They were now allowed to vote and, a few years later, would participate in deciding whether Little Falls would become a wet or dry town.

There were continual conflicts among the residents about whether the saloons should remain open on

Sundays, be closed part of the day or be completely closed. It was a hot topic at the local saloons. The Como brothers and some friends were discussing this very subject at the Leblanc saloon one evening.

"Did you read the article in this Friday's paper about the petition submitted to the Mayor requesting that saloons be closed on Sundays?" Felix asked in disgust.

"Yes, those old biddies are just trying to initiate trouble. We all know who they are; they're always opposing what the majority of residents want. They presented the Mayor with a petition, but they couldn't even solicit enough signatures to make it legitimate. It's a joke," Arthur added.

"I like the Mayor's response... 'if a person should keep wine at his house and give a glass to a visiting friend on Sunday he would be liable to arrest and fine, and he did not see how wine could be disposed of at church communion without violating this law.' That was funny, I thought," Felix snickered.

"Yes, what a bunch of crap," voiced Del Leblanc as he slid another beer down the bar to Arthur. "This is my business and two old bags are not going to stop me from running my business, when and how I see fit. It's none of their business.

"Well, thank goodness our Mayor has the sense to shut them up," Felix remarked.

"He even took the time to discuss their proposal with the Clergy and the Saloon owners, and none of them expressed the need to close saloons on Sundays. Mayor Richardson is a good, and fair Mayor," Arthur responded.

"And very respectful for not interfering with our business," added Del.

Life in Little Falls became quite enjoyable for the Como brothers, while the saloons remained open. They were working in logging camps or at the sawmills and making ends meet. They bought homes in the same neighbourhood, on the same side of the river, so their children could play together and go to the same schools. Their wives were busy raising numerous children. Between the four families of Felix, Oney, Omer, and Virginie, there were twenty-eight cousins. Only two children, both Virginie's and Julien's, had died shortly after birth. Life seemed almost perfect.

Chapter 20

Little Falls, Minnesota - 1898

The years 1898 and 1899 proved to be cataclysmic for the Como families.

First, a fire nearly destroyed Felix's house. It had started at Heroux's barn next door. When the fire department arrived, three buildings and a woodshed had caught on fire. Felix's house, immediately east of where the fire originated, had just started to burn. When the fire was finally doused and put out, Felix's residence had been saved but sustained approximately one hundred dollars of damage. All the other buildings were destroyed. In the Heroux barn, a stallion belonging to Mr. Heroux and a cow belonging to Felix had both perished in the flames.

The tragic events that followed in 1899, are extremely difficult to write about. Little Falls experienced a devastating diphtheria outbreak. Felix and Marie's home was the first Como household to become infected. In late March their eight year old daughter died from diphtheria. A three year old daughter, initially diagnosed with bronchitis, had died four days earlier. She had attended school claiming that she "only had a sore throat" to her mother. Because the doctor believed it to be bronchitis, several friends and relatives along with their children went to the house to view the remains of the little girl and pay their respect. It was only when the second child became ill and died that they suspected something much more contagious. It is obvious why the epidemic had spread so quickly and infiltrated all the other Como households.

Julien and Virginie's house was quarantined when their five year old daughter, Alma, became ill. The State Board of Health had mandated a four-week quarantine for diphtheria patients. Before the quarantine order could be lifted, a regulated bacteriological examination with two negative reports was necessary.

Alma died shortly after.

In March, Dr. Dumont was treating Oney Como's family. One by one, their children had become infected.

"Your children are all improving," he told Oney's wife, Leonie. "They are practically out of danger now."

The optimism of the doctor was reassuring and comforting to Leonie.

"Thank goodness! I'm so glad to hear that Doctor. But I think I am going to need help to nurse them back to complete health. I can't do this alone with just my two oldest boys. I am working around the clock and I'm exhausted. I wish Oney could be here to help."

Shortly after, nurse Phoebe Boynton was placed on duty full-time at Oney's house. The circumstances had suddenly become dire. The Doctor's judgement on the situation had been grossly underestimated. Six of their eight children were gravely ill. On May 12, 1899, the Little Falls Herald reported:

'Mr. and Mrs. O Como lost another child – the fourth within three weeks last Monday evening. The last to die was a boy 8 years old. The child died of exhaustion, after an attack of diphtheria. The funeral was private. This makes six [recte, five] children in the family who have died, another is still sick.'[7]

Within a few weeks, all six children died. This disease was known as the children's plague because of the high death rate among children under five years old and characterized as 'The Strangling Angel of Children'. As the disease progressed the toxins produced by the bacteria created a thick film in the throat that made it difficult to breathe. Ultimately the thick film strangled the patient to death.

Virginie and Julien lost another four children, while Felix and Marie lost two daughters and two sons. Of the twenty-eight cousins, only fourteen remained. At the time, Oney and Felix, were in Bemidji working as carpenters. When the tragic news of a diphtheria outbreak in their homes reached them, the grief-stricken fathers returned to Little Falls for the funerals.

Miss Boynton's bill totalling $34 for her services as a nurse for the Como family was submitted to the city council. In council, the probable allowance for this bill was debated at length. Some of the councillors believed that Mr. Como could meet this obligation, so it was first tabled but eventually, it was paid by the city.

The newspapers were not only filled with tragic stories of complete families being wiped out in just a few hours from diphtheria, but also congested with ads offering preposterous claims of potions to instantly kill the disease:

'Mull's Lightning Pain Killer instantly kills Cholera, Croup, Rheumatism, Diphtheria or any other pain internal or external. 25c. Safe for children, absolutely pure. For sale by M. V. Wetzel.'[8]

There were others who believed that diphtheria could be cured by faith healers:

'Another Victim of Faith Cure.
A child in Le Sueur is treated by a Dowieite and dies of diphtheria. Courts will act.'[9]

'Two Chrisitan Science "healers" are on trial in Minneapolis. They treated a child for diphtheria.'[10]

The summer following the diphtheria outbreak, Omer and Oney left Little Falls to work for the Weyerhaeuser Nebagamon Lumber Company in Wisconsin. Tall timbers, water, good transportation and a nearby metropolitan area, were exactly what Frederick Weyerhaeuser needed for an ideal lumber mill location.

The mill at Lake Nebagamon was founded in 1899 and it attracted a large number of thirsty lumbermen. Twenty-eight saloons popped up over a very short time. As in other regions, saloon owners found themselves in the midst of the same continual harassment. It seemed that populations everywhere were conflicted over the sale of strong spirituous, malt, ardent and intoxicating liquors. The town boards were continually revoking licenses and charging saloon owners for opening on Sundays, for selling liquor to persons on the 'black list' and for harbouring gambling on the premises.

Next a break-and-enter occurred at Felix's home and was reported in the Little Falls Herald:

'A young man named Ole Knudson was arrested on Monday. He had been attempting to force an entrance to the dwelling house of Mr. Como on First street and Second avenue northeast, and the family was aroused and the police called. At first it was thought that it was an attempt at burglary, but later it was found that Knudson was on the verge of the 'jim jams' having been drinking hard for some time and was hardly responsible for his actions at the time...'[11]

At least nothing was taken and no one was hurt. The young man was charged for being drunk and disorderly conduct, and fined ten dollars.

A few months later, Oney was back home in Little Falls for another of his child's funeral, the seventh that year. The December issue of the Little Falls Herald reported this tragedy, in part as follows:

'River Gets One Victim

Two Boys Through the Ice While Skating Monday Evening and One is Drowned

... All Monday afternoon when the river between the two bridges was covered with skaters, and among them were two boys, Joseph Como and Ed King. They were skating just opposite the Pine Tree saw mill not far from the boom at about 5:30 when the ice gave way and both were precipitated into the water. Other boys were close at hand, but they were powerless to render aid to the two unfortunate boys who were struggling in the water for their lives. Their cries, however, soon attracted the attention of J.A. Foss and Matt Roberts, who live near the bank of the river, where the boys had fallen in. The cries were readily understood and by rare presence of mind one of them secured a plank and they ran to the rescue. When they reached them, only one boy could be seen. He was clinging to the ice, but it was evident that he would soon have lost his hold for he was rapidly becoming benumbed by the very cold water in which he was almost wholly submerged...

The drowned boy was ten years old and the son of Mr. and Mrs. O. Como, who live on First Street and 5th Avenue Northeast, just a few rods from the river's edge and almost opposite the spot where their son lost his life.

It is the same family from which four [*recte*, six] children were taken last spring from diphtheria, and there is now but one child remaining out of a family of six [*recte*, eight]. Surely the unhappy family's cup of sorrow is filled to overflowing. Deep sympathy for the afflicted parents is expressed by everyone, and especially for the mother. She is here alone, her husband being away Lake Nebagamon, Wis., at work at his trade of carpentry on the Weyerhaeuser saw mill at that place.

He was telegraphed immediately and answered that he would come on the first train.

Mrs. Como was completely prostrated with grief when the news of her son's death was conveyed to her and she has been under the physician's care ever since...'[12]

~~~~~~

It was the last year of the nineteenth century, 1899. Oney and Leonie had lost seven children that year. Only the oldest child, a twelve-year-old boy, remained. The following February, Leonie gave birth to a little girl.

Shortly after these traumatic events unfolded, my great Uncle Oney was reported in the Duluth News-Tribune to have disappeared for some time, and was believed to be unwell. His family thought he had checked into the Duluth Hospital. However, he never arrived at the hospital. He was later found in Port Arthur (Thunder Bay), Canada, carrying a large sum of money, disoriented and unaware of where or who he was. It isn't surprising that one's state of mind might be foggy and lacking clarity after these traumatic events. Most likely, he had developed post-traumatic stress disorder. Thinking of my seven children losing one would have been devastating: but losing all seven in just a few months would have been crippling! In French there is a saying: *"elle avait les jambes molles comme de la guenille"*. It means that when you are entirely distraught from emotional trauma, your knees go weak, and your legs go limp like a rag. I pictured my grand Aunt on her knees, weeping for days, unable to stand on her legs.

Meanwhile, the Comos continued to provide for their families wherever the work was available. After a couple of years in Wisconsin, Oney had moved to Hibbing, MN and had recruited Arthur to work for him with the boom crew. The crew worked on the water at the log pond sorting the logs and assembling them into rafts for shipment. The job required the boom tender to walk on the floating logs, moving dexterously from one to another. The work was laborious and dangerous, but Arthur enjoyed working for his brother.

During this time the Saskatchewan Valley Land Co. of St. Paul, the largest land company in the United States handling Canadian lands, promised one thousand-quarter sections of rich fertile land in the Saskatchewan Valley. The newspaper ads titled FREE FARMS IN WESTERN CANADA made it seem like a walk-in-the-park profession compared to the difficult work in the logging industry. In 1902, Felix, travelled with a large party of locals to Saskatchewan to check out the farmland. But he returned unimpressed. He was not going to give up his trade in the lumber business to become a farmer. Omer, on the other hand, after listening carefully to Felix's trip details, was enthused. The abundance of farmland and the change of lifestyle appealed to him. He soon abandoned the logging industry and moved north of the line. In 1903, Omer and his family arrived at La Plaine, Saskatchewan, a community northeast of Rosthern, where he homesteaded until his death in 1924. He returned to Little Falls thirteen years after his move to visit his brothers, Felix, Arthur, and his sister Virginie.

~~~~~~

Was it coincidental that I would be born in Hoey, Saskatchewan, only fifty kilometres from where my grand uncle, Omer, would end up homesteading? And that his granddaughter, Armande Fauchoux (Como) and I would connect in the 90s and become very close friends. Perhaps the immediate strong bond we developed was because we shared a great-grandfather: Elzear.

Our friendship endured for several decades. Not only did Armande and her husband Vic winter in Mesa, Arizona with us for many years, but we also travelled extensively together. We spent over a month together in Mexico in a small camper, but we never felt cramped or crowded. We were always so comfortable with each other. Another time, again with our small camper, we travelled across Canada to Nova Scotia to attend the World Acadian Congress in 2004. It was a wonderful reunion of Comeau Cousins from all over the world.

Chapter 21

Little Falls, Minnesota – 1901

In 1901, after eleven years in Little Falls, at the age of twenty-six and now a full US citizen, Arthur returned to Quebec to visit his mother and sister. He made a stop on his way to Nashua, New Hampshire, where his brother Albert, a painter by trade, was living with his family. The following year, Arthur returned to Quebec again, but this time is was on a wife-hunting expedition. Minnesota was full of men, almost twice as many men as women, and Arthur knew that the pickings were slim. He had looked around in Little Falls, but there were no females of interest. However, there were plenty of eligible French Catholic women back home, like the Bergeron girls. Arthur's brother, Albert, had married Marie Bergeron, and Arthur had his eye on her sister, Delphine Bergeron. After three weeks in Canada, Arthur and Delphine were married on October 28 in Inverness, Quebec.

This was Arthur's last visit home to Quebec. His mother and sister would never again see Arthur, nor would they ever meet his children. Francoise remained in Quebec with her daughter, Rosana, until she passed away in 1906. Her son Albert and two sons-in-law, Joseph Bourque (Melanie Comeau) and Victor Cormier (Leah Comeau), were present at her funeral. Rosana moved to Sainte-Angele-de Laval, where she worked as a seamstress. She was never married. She died at the age of forty-one, on December 18, 1917; her brother Albert was present at her burial.

When newly married Arthur and Delphine returned to Little Falls, they purchased a home, and settled in. On October 10, 1903, my father, Harry Como Sr. was born. He was baptized eight days later with godparents Julien & Virginie (Como) Richards in attendance. The first few years of his life were uneventful. Delphine had an uncomplicated pregnancy and a quick delivery. Harry was a good baby and an only child for fifteen months.

Just like clockwork, Como babies were born every other year. Norman came along in 1905; his godparents were Felix and Marie Como, his aunt and uncle. Ena was born June 8, 1907; her godparents were cousins, Marie Anne Richards, Virginie Como's daughter and her husband, Eugene Heroux. Clarence, a third son, born in August 1909, was baptized Joseph Albert Clarence. His godparents were Albert Como, Felix's son, and Prima Richards, Virginie's daughter. They were his cousins, both single adults in their early twenties. Father Lamothe officiated the baptisms for the Como babies at St. Francis Xavier Church. Until 1914, they were a family of six.

By 1907, Arthur had given up his career in the logging industry to appease Delphine and be closer to home while the children were young. Instead, he had taken a bartending position at the Leblanc Saloon, located on Broadway East and owned by brothers Dell Leblanc and Robert Leblanc, whose ancestors also hailed from Acadia. The Leblancs, like the Doucets, had immigrated to Minnesota in the mid to late 1880s and were well-established.

The Como family had become well-known in the community. Arthur was well-liked as the barkeeper of an establishment that served alcohol to his many friends, family, and residents of Little Falls. But the career change from logging camps to saloon bartender did not make Delphine happier. While Arthur was no longer away for long periods, he was still seldom home. The barkeeper's hours kept him away most days between 5 pm till closing so he was rarely home for the children's bedtime.

The Leblanc Saloon was the establishment that the Como brothers, their friends, and co-workers favoured and would congregate whenever they were in town on a break from the logging camps. As barkeeper, Arthur was responsible for closing the business every night and usually came home very late. He prided himself on his appearance and his drink-pouring abilities. He would pour a few heavy-handed drinks throughout the evening and often came home intoxicated.

One evening, when Arthur was bartending, a man he did not recognize came in and sat at the bar. He ordered a drink, and they had a short conversation. It was a usual weeknight with the familiar crowd and commotion.

"Hey, are you closing up the bar tonight? and at what time?" the man asked Arthur.

"I'm closing up at 11:00."

After several drinks, the man got up and left the saloon.

Arthur closed up the saloon, arrived at home and went to bed as usual. Shortly before one o'clock in the morning, Delphine awoke startled!

"What's that noise"? she whispered, as she shook Arthur to wake him up.

Quickly, he sat up in bed and listened attentively for a few minutes. All was quiet.

"There's no one there! Go back to sleep," he reassured Delphine.

He fell back asleep, but Delphine was not convinced and laid awake. She had definitely heard something, but she wasn't sure whether the noise came from inside the house or from outside.

"AAAAAAAAAAH!" Delphine screamed as she clutched her blanket. The sound that came out of her mouth could be heard two blocks away. She had witnessed a figure moving in the kitchen. Her shrilling scream startled the intruder, and he ran past their bedroom and out the front door. Arthur immediately got up to check the house and the yard. The intruder was gone. There didn't seem to be anything missing. The cash was still safely tucked away in the hiding spot. Delphine was shaken up and ran to the children's bedroom. She was relieved that they had not even stirred during the commotion. Thank goodness she had gotten a good glimpse of the man when he ran by their bedroom and was able to provide the police with an accurate description.

"He was wearing a blue shirt, no hat. I don't think he was wearing any shoes either. He appeared to be in his stocking feet," she reported, still very frightened from the previous night's episode.

Arthur was certain that he was the man he had talked to the previous evening at the saloon.

That same evening, just an hour later, the police had been alerted to another incident of break and enter. This invasion was at the home of another bartender, who had had a similar visit in his saloon. He had also been asked the question: "Will you be closing the saloon this evening?" With a second similar description of a man in a blue shirt, wearing slippers, the police were convinced it was the same man. The robber was aware that whoever closed up the saloon at the end of the shift would be bringing home the cash for safekeeping. The amount would often exceed two hundred dollars, making it a profitable venture for a thief. Arthur and Delphine were relieved that, other than the trauma of the attempted burglary, there was nothing of value taken, and the three little ones sleeping in the room next door had not heard a thing. Little Ena was just over a month old.

~~~~~~

It must have been a stressful time in my grandmother's life, dealing with my grandfather's choice of profession, drinking, and the characters he was mingling with. Hearing about petty thievery reminds me of the story of Jean Valjean, who was forced to steal to survive. For the most part, I have always believed that people are fundamentally good, and if someone wanted to steal from me it was because they needed whatever they were attempting to steal more than me. My children called me naïve, but I found it easier to accept the good in humanity rather than the evil.

I am not foolish enough to think that greed and power don't exist. There is corruption in every sector of society. Heads of State, Government and Political leaders, and the Churches, have all exerted their muscles in the name of power and greed. Canada is no exception. Throughout its short history, every ethnicity in Canada has experienced prejudices, discrimination and oppression. Why? Because they were not of English descent. The Acadians, the Indigenous People, and many of the immigrants from Germany, Austria, Hungary, Bulgaria, and the Ottoman Empire who were labelled as enemy aliens during WWI, to name a few, suffered tremendous hardships. Each criminality has left deep and painful scars on many of the people of Canada.

Les maudits Anglais! The damn English! If you weren't one of them, you were persecuted!

Chapter 22

Little Falls, Minnesota – 1910

Arthur and Delphine's family grew up at 400 – 4th Street NE in Little Falls. It was a good-sized, one-and-a-half-story family home, located on a corner lot, the South 1/2 of Lot 4, Block 58. Delphine loved it.

It was in this house that the tradition of storytelling continued, and the Como children heard the infamous bedtime tales about their ancestors. On the few nights that Arthur was home to help get the children off to bed, they would beg him for a story.

"Which story do you want to hear tonight," Arthur asked.

Harry, 7, and Norman, 5, quickly positioned themselves at their father's knees. Each child wanted a different story.

"Mutiny on the Pembroke," Harry commanded.

"Cat-O-Nine-Tails Whipping story," Norman countered.

"NO, NO, I want Simon Says," three-year-old Ena cried as she came running in dragging her cloth doll, who's embroidered mouth had been kissed off. She quickly climbed on Arthur's lap to claim the best seat. She was Arthur's little girl, and he almost always gave in to her wishes.

"Ok, Ok," Arthur began without hesitation:

"Simon Comeau and his family loved their land in Acadia. They called it the country of happiness and serenity. They knew that they would be miserable anywhere else on earth because in Acadia, there was always enough food to fill their bellies. Acadia, they said, was Paradise on Earth.

One day the British Governor came to Simon and says: Simon, you and your family have to leave Acadia.

Simon says: But why? We love Acadia.

The King of England wants this land for his people. He does not want Acadians on this land.

Simon says: But where shall we go?

The King wants you to go to Virginia.

So, Simon and his family boarded a ship and sailed down the coast to Virginia.

When they arrived in Virginia the Governor says: Why are all these people coming here? We were not told that we were getting all these people. We do not want these people here. You cannot stay here.

Simon says: Then where shall we go?

The Governor says: I don't know. I will ask the King. Stay here until the King decides.

Four months later the Governor returned and says: You must go to England.

Simon says: We don't want to go to England. We want to go to Acadia.

But it is the King's wish for you to go to England, and that is where you shall go.

So, Simon and his family boarded another ship and sailed across the ocean to England.

When they arrived the British Governor says: Why are all these people coming here? We were not told that we were getting all these people. We do not want these people here.

Simon says: Then where shall we go?

I don't know. I will ask the King. Stay here until the King decides.

Two weeks later the Governor returned and says: The King of England will allow you to stay here.

Simon says: But we do not want to stay here. How long must we stay here?

I don't know; I will ask the King. Stay here until the King decides when you can leave.

Seven years later the Governor returned and says: You may leave now; the King of England does not want you here anymore.

Simon says: Where shall we go?

The King wants you to go to France. It is your home.

Simon says: We don't want to go to France! It is not our home. We want to go to Acadia. That is our home.

No, you cannot go to Acadia. The King says Acadia belongs to the English people now! The King does not want you there.

So, Simon and his family boarded another ship and sailed across the English Channel to France.

When they arrived the French Lieutenant says: Why are all these people coming here? We don't want all these people. We cannot look after all these people.

Simon says: So what shall we do?

The King of France says you must stay here.

Twenty-two years later the Lieutenant came to Simon and says: The King says you can leave now!

Simon says: Where shall we go?

A ship will come soon to take you to Haiti or to Spanish Louisiana if you wish.

So, Simon and his family boarded another ship and sailed across the ocean to Haiti.

They did not like Haiti.

Soon after Simon and his family boarded another ship and went to Spanish Louisiana.

For thirty years they had been bounced around from the shores of eastern Canada to Virginia USA, to Bristol, England to St Malo, France to Mirebalais, Haiti, and finally to Opelousas, Louisiana. Louisiana was the closest place they had been to in a very, very long time that felt like home. But it was not their beloved land of Acadia, the country of happiness and serenity, a place they would never return to again. The end."

Ena contemplated the story for a minute.

"But why couldn't they go back?" she asked inquisitively.

"They weren't allowed," Arthur responded. "The King of England had taken all the Acadians land and had given it to the British, English people. The British now called Acadia, Nova Scotia. There was no more Acadia and the British did not want Acadians to come back and live there."

"But why couldn't they all live together?"

Ena's three year old mind would not quit asking 'why'?? questions. As difficult as it was to explain, Arthur always took the extra time to talk about the expulsion and how families were affected.

The Acadians had a rich tradition of storytelling. The stories were not folktales or legends but true historical accounts of what had happened to their ancestors during the great upheaval. They were transmitted orally and passed down through the generations. Sometimes the facts had been dramatized or exaggerated slightly, but only so they could add some enjoyment and entertainment for the children. From these stories, they would learn about the historical events that transpired during the Great Upheaval in 1755.

Little Falls was a great community for the children; there was always someone to hang out with and always something to do. Harry, Norman, and their cousins, the children of Felix and Virginia, spent their adolescent years playing outside. The street was their playground, and just beyond everyone's backyard were the back alleys. These recreation areas were the center of their social activities, the treasure trove of their youth. The alleyways were dirty, contained garbage, paint cans, rope, broken tools, and discarded items free for the taking. Rummaging for abandoned or discarded stuff no one wanted was their favourite pastime, and they would often haul their newly discovered treasures home.

The Mississippi River, only a few blocks away from their home, provided hours of entertainment. Daily outings to the banks, where they fished, played with the turtles basking on the warm rocks and foraged amongst the aspen, chokecherries and willows. The river was a mysterious place to their young minds; it awakened their curiosity and excited their imaginations. Nature was also their playground; it was unscripted, outdoor free play where they could stomp through puddles and muck, climb trees and explore flora and fauna.

One afternoon the Como boys were out scrummaging at the river and came upon some good wood. Imagine what they could build with it! A raft, a treehouse? Next thing you know, the Hennepin Paper Company filed complaints against the Como families. They claimed to have lost considerable wood, taken from the river. The wood, bearing the Company's mark, was found in several yards, including Felix and Virginie's yards. In court, Felix and Julian, Virginie's husband, maintained that they did not know where the wood came from and, if any was taken, the children brought it without their consent or knowledge. They were absolved from paying a six dollar fine.

The Como cousins were good boys and did not get into too much mischief. The worst thing that ever happened was that they came home with torn trousers and scraped knees. And while they spent their days gallivanting outdoors, Ena, like most young girls, spent her time indoors with her mother learning how to cook, sew, and help with domestic chores. Occasionally she would raid her mother's sewing basket for scraps of fabric, buttons, and lace to make clothing for her dolls. The kids had great adventures in their early years. But despite being deprived of toys, they always found something to do and something to play with.

Chapter 23

Harry

Like my father and his siblings, I did not have many toys, but I recall getting a dog named Collie. My cousins, the Guigons, had given him to me, and I spent many hours after my chores were finished training him to pull me in my makeshift wagon. Once the dog got tired, I would make him jump into the wagon, and I would give him a ride. We spent many hours together; he was a good companion.

Even though the 1930s were years of depression, we always managed to find something to entertain ourselves with. My uncle Hippolyte was a craftsman when it came to woodworking. He was highly skilled at making musical instruments and board games for his children. I lived only a quarter of a mile away, so I was able to spend many winter days at their home enjoying the flatpicking guitar and fiddle sessions. Uncle gave me one of his prized handcrafted guitars, still in my possession today, and a keepsake that will be passed on to future generations. Handcrafted from a variety of locally sourced woods, it has small inlaid triangles around the guitar's edge, stained a darker brown. I can still clearly see his pencilled signature in the soundhole:

1945
Hyppolite Guigon
Hoey, Sask.

I also spent many hours playing checkers and Nine Man's Morris. The two games, built on opposite sides of an 18" x 18" square wooden box, were inlaid with intricate pieces of wood and contained two little pull-out drawers at each end for the checkers. Another treasure to be passed down.

In 1940, there was one thing that my brother and I desired most. It was a bicycle! We hounded our mother endlessly. My thirteen-year-old brother also wanted a rifle. After all, what thirteen-year-old boy on the farm did not own a rifle? By that age, it was a rite of passage. When my mother asked us to sign a promissory note for the bicycle, I was ten years old. She was finally giving in if we agreed to her terms.

The contract made us promise to be obedient, say our prayers morning and night, kneel very straight, to not fight, to love one another, and ask God each day for his grace to become better, to always love him more, take good care of our clothing, to do what's asked of us quickly and without hesitation, to be honest, to not go to bed later than nine o'clock, to awake immediately when called and to not go out without permission and unnecessarily. In a single word, be good Christians, good children, to treat others as you would want to be treated.

As an aside note, it stated that we were to read only good books and to be done with silly ideas about getting a rifle (*pas d'idees de carabine – fini ça*). Enough was enough!

Of course, we agreed and happily signed. We spent many hours enjoying our new bicycle. The original promissory note is still in my possession today.

Chapter 24

Little Falls, Minnesota – 1911

Felix moved his family to Tacoma, Washington where he had taken a position as a millwright with the North End Lumber Company in 1911. It was a small mill producing eight to fifteen million board feet annually. Meanwhile, Oney was in Fort William (Thunder Bay), Ontario, Canada with his small family, employed as a carpenter/housebuilder. And in Rosthern Saskatchewan, Canada, Omer was busy homesteading, clearing land and also a house builder for the large Mennonite community.

Arthur was still in the business of mixing drinks, but not at the Leblanc saloon. By 1909, the 6500 residents of Little Falls had twenty-three saloons to choose from to quench their thirsts. Ten of these watering holes were within three blocks on East Broadway, and this gave

Arthur his pick of establishments to pursue his trade. He had been hired to manage John Dolan's saloon on East Broadway. John Dolan, a bachelor Irishman, had arrived in Little Falls via Virginia in about 1884. His saloon had been operational for over twenty-five years when he decided to retire. Since Arthur was so well-liked in the community, John believed Arthur would be an excellent candidate to operate the saloon and handed him the keys.

In 1912 the title of the house that Delphine so loved was transferred to Charles A. Lindbergh for $450. Lindbergh, whose son, Charles Augustus Lindbergh, would become a famous aviator, had established a practice in Little Falls, and quickly became one of the town's leading citizens. Serving as the county attorney, he acquired a lot of land around the Little Falls region. He was elected to the US House of Representatives in 1906, a position he held for ten years.

Arthur moved his family out of their home and into a two-room apartment above the saloon. The family of six was now living in a cramped one-bedroom apartment directly above the saloon, a well-patronized watering hole for many folks of questionable reputation. There was always a stench of stale whiskey, beer, and smoke permeating the floor of their apartment. The fistfights, swearing, yelling, and constant commotion below were not conducive to raising a family of young children. It was not the type of life Delphine had envisioned for herself and her children. They were barely making ends meet, and Delphine worried incessantly about Arthur's excessive drinking. She was also always fearful of another robbery.

Arthur's drinking only got worse as time passed on. When he first started bartending, the drinking was under control; he was young and had the stamina to get drunk every night and maintain normalcy with work and family life. Like most alcoholics, he was in denial. He took pride in the fact that he could carry on with the management of the saloon business while handling large quantities of alcohol without any severe hangovers or blackouts. He rarely got visibly drunk. He had attempted to quit several times but never succeeded. He would always rationalize: "It's been a tough day; I'll quit tomorrow," and then he would pour himself a stiff one.

Eight months later, the saloon closed. Arthur was out of work, and Delphine was expecting their fifth child.

Perhaps it was Arthur's excessive drinking that led to the saloon closure and perhaps it was because of the owner's health that had taken a turn for the worst and he was desperate to sell the business. The saloon, along with the complete Dolan brick block situated on Broadway East, were quickly advertised for sale. Arthur was of course in no position to purchase it; he could barely afford his rent and food for his family. But the saloon closure had only been temporary. The business did not sell as quickly as John Dolan wished, so he recruited a new manager to operate the saloon and re-opened it. When the sale was finalized John returned to West Virginia to be with his family and died shortly afterwards.

That year, in 1915, a new law passed that allowed the counties to call special elections on the liquor question by collecting signatures from area voters. The Little Falls Herald posted the following in the February 19th edition:

'SHALL CITY BE WET OR DRY?

Petition Circulated To Submit Question To Voters At the Spring Election

On March 16, the day of the general election, the citizens of Little Falls will be given an opportunity to voice their will as to whether this city shall continue to have saloons. A petition has been circulated this week and will be filed with the city clerk today or tomorrow, asking for a vote on the question. The petition now contains over 100 names, which is more than 10 per cent required, and will likely bear 150 signatures before it is filed. F.A. Nelson is at the head of the movement.

Dry workers claim that they have a chance of winning. Considerable interest is being manifested in the matter.

Should citizens vote to put Little Falls on the dry map, the eighteen saloons would be closed as soon as the vote is canvassed. A separate ballot will be required to vote on the question.'[13]

The question on the ballot was simple: Shall the sale of liquor be prohibited? Forty-five of the fifty counties in Minnesota had opted to go dry, but Morrison County, consisting of twenty-one townships, including Little Falls, was not amongst them. Bartending had been Arthur's livelihood, so all of his friends and relatives had voted for the Wetside and they won!

Unfortunately, this outcome was not a favourable one for Arthur's family. The saloons in Little Falls remained open, and Arthur continued to drink, patronizing his favourite establishments.

Unexpectedly, at the age of forty-three, Arthur passed away at his home in Little Falls from heart trouble after a brief illness. It's what the newspaper reported, however, three days before his death, Arthur decided to stop drinking cold turkey! He had been a chronic alcoholic for many years, and the sudden withdrawal from alcohol caused a rapid onset of confusion and uncontrollable shaking. On February 23, 1917, he died from delirium tremens. The Obituary in the Little Falls Herald read:

'DIED

Arthur Como, aged 43 years, passed away Friday at his home here from heart trouble after a brief illness.

Deceased was born in St. Angele de Laval, Canada, March 4, 1874. On Oct 28, 1902, he was married to Miss Delphine Bergeron, in Canada. Mr. Como was a resident of this city for about twenty-eight years.

Surviving the deceased are his wife and five children, Harry, Normand, Ena, Clarence and Lories [*recte* Louis].

The funeral was held Sunday afternoon at 4 o'clock from St. Francis Xavier church, Father Lamothe officiating. Interment was in Calvary cemetery.'[14]

The January 1918 issue of the Little Falls Herald column titled 'Happenings of the Past Year – Review of Events that are important to Morrison County People' recapped the most unusual and high-profile events that had occurred in 1917. Starting with five arrests for rowdyism on New Year's Eve, the write-up continued with liquor violations and local wholesale liquor dealers violating the Indian Liquor Lid to arrests for accidentals, typical small town break and enters, burglaries and accidental shootings. It listed the number of drafted men from the county who left for Camp Dodge, an army base in Johnson, Iowa. And of course, the column would not be complete without reporting on the extreme weather conditions throughout the year. A blizzard in January dumped seven inches of snow in the city. There was another in February and one in March which almost completely halted traffic on the LF&D line (Little Falls and Dakota Railroad Company). Towns along this rail line were snowbound for weeks. In July, the thermometer recorded a high of 104 degrees Fahrenheit, the hottest day in over twenty years. Then came heavy windstorms in August which flattened many buildings in the county, ending with a light earthquake in September that lasted only half a minute. The deaths of all the well-known persons in the county, including the death of Arthur Como, completed the year in review section.

Delphine was left heartbroken and destitute. She had five children, including a three-year-old son, Louis. She would question for the rest of her life: What if the residents had voted for a dry town and the saloons would have closed? Would Arthur have found other meaningful employment? Would he have been forced to abstain from drinking?

He died when his children were still so young.

Delphine moved her family to 611 Third Street Southeast. It was a large one and one-half storey house with dormers on the front and south side, and a large enclosed front veranda facing west. They shared the rental property with another family: Samuel and Amy Holtslander and their young son.

Delphine worked tirelessly as a seamstress accepting odd tailoring jobs to make ends meet. During the war, it had been considered a highly valued talent and had become a popular home craft to provide women with a means to contribute to the household economy. It was during this time that Delphine had honed her skills of fine tailoring and developed a passion for the industry. She was self-taught, but eventually became very accomplished. She had a keen eye for fit, form and function, and a knack for repurposing old clothing into something new and beautiful. She spent all day at her sewing machine until her back and neck ached. After the children were in bed, she devoted her nights to stitching fine details on garments by hand until her eyes were red and sore from the strain of working in poor lighting conditions. But she was able to support her family. They had no other income or savings until Harry found employment.

~~~~~~

I remember my grandmother Delphine being a wonderful seamstress. For my first year of school, I lived with her in Bellevue. My mother was concerned that because of my small stature and timid nature, it would be best for me to live with her, close to the school. That year Grandma sewed me a beautiful Melton wool winter coat. The wool cloth had been well fulled, making it thick, fuzzy and warm. It was grey, double-breasted, mid-calf and had a quilted lining. The tailoring and overstitched edges were immaculate. It fitted me perfectly. She was also very good at weaving and made beautiful, colourful rugs from rags on her loom.

My father, Harry Sr. was significantly affected by the death of his father. Delphine, now the sole provider for the family, struggled to make ends meet. Wanting to help his mother with the financial burden, Harry at sixteen years old, began working as a labourer in a flour mill.

While lumber sawmills had arrived first in Minnesota, they were quickly overtaken by the flour mills. Flour mills outlasted the sawmilling industry by several decades. There were several mills in operation in Little Falls, and they provided jobs for young boys such as a sack boy, whose job would be to move the sacks about the mills and add empty sacks to the chutes when ones filled up. The mills produced flour under such brand names as Gold Dust and King of Minnesota. For more than half a century, nearby Minneapolis was known as the Flour Milling Capital of the World. In addition to helping contribute to the household expenses, the work helped Harry take his mind off his father's death and cope with his suffering.

Delphine made the best of their living situation. The children were resilient and continued to excel at school. They attended Hawthorne School in English, and after school Delphine taught them French, to ensure their French heritage would not be forgotten or lost.

During those school years, the agricultural extension division of the University of Minnesota was developing the Boys and Girls Clubs throughout the State of

Minnesota. The Bread Club, Canning Club, Garment Club, Pig Club, Calf club, and Potato Club, to name a few, provided extra-curricular activities for children in the area where the Como children were often enrolled.

The participating schools in each county would compete, and the winners would be sent to the State Fair, all expenses paid. Eleven-year-old Ena Como belonged to the Bread Club and she was thankful the war had ended along with the flour rations. The newspaper ads alerting Minnesotans on flour restrictions were enough to scare anyone into abandoning all baking. Hoarding was not allowed!

'To the People of Minnesota:

The Federal Food Administration hereby requires everyone who has more than thirty days' supply of wheat flour to return the flour at once to the dealer or miller from whom it was purchased or report to his County Food Administrator. The order applies to everyone no matter when or how the flour was obtained. Thirty days' supply is determined on the basis of 6 lbs. for each member of the household.....'

The ad assured people that if they presently had an excess of flour on hand, that did not automatically make them a hoarder.... and that in normal times it would suggest that they were thrifty and sensible buyers and not feel in any way that they had done something wrong. The need for flour was a condition of war and the Allies were desperate for food.

'Bread they must have and bread we must furnish...'

The last paragraph of the ad warned them of the consequences of hoarding:

'Anyone who insists on keeping more than one month's supply or is using more than 6 lbs per person per month is considered a hoarder and will be dealt with accordingly. Hoarding of necessary foods is punishable by a fine of $5,000 or imprisonment for two years or both.'[15]

Now that there were no longer scares regarding using flour, an upcoming bread competition had excited Ena.

"Mom, Mom," she called out. "The competition is on next weekend. I have baked six times, so I qualify, and I want to compete. Can we practice today?"

"There's lots of time, Ena," Delphine replied. "We will try a batch tomorrow morning. First, check and make sure we have everything. Read me the details in the newspaper:"

'Dear Club workers:
The bread contests will be held Friday and Saturday at the high school at 10 o'clock. Friday for the Lincoln, Columbia and Central schools. Saturday for the Parochial and Hawthorne schools. The secretary of each club must notify the members who are eligible for the contest. Each one should bring:
1 dish towel
1-6 cups of barley flour

2 ½ cups white flour
1 dish cloth
1 potato
Please be sure to notify all in your clubs who have baked six times.
Sincerely
Susan A. Hough
Home Demonstration Agent'[16]

An afternoon of baking and testing would always guarantee a huge mess! Had a bag of flour exploded? No, but there was enough white powder floating in the air that Ena appeared to be baking in a snow globe! Although she baked her heart out, she did not win the first competition she entered. But she tried again the following year, practicing even harder at home with her mother. Delphine was an excellent breadmaker; this was another area in which she was highly skilled. Her artisan bread had a memorable flavour and aroma, a fluffy interior and a perfectly baked golden crust. It was a buttery pleasure to bite into a slice. She was confident with a little more practice, Ena could also master the skill and become a 'breadwinner'.

For the next competition, contestants were required to have made yeast bread at least nine times and quick breads three times. They were also required to keep a record of the work and to write a story about breadmaking. She was so excited to read the results in the newspaper.

"Mom, I won at my school!" she exclaimed. "Look,

Alma and I won for our school. Our names are in the newspaper."

But she did not win at the county level.

The following year, cake making, a supplementary project to the bread-making contest was introduced. It was for bread-making club members only, based on the butter loaf cake. It would be held at the same time as the bread-making contest. A story on "My Cake and What I Learned in Cake Making" needed to be submitted before the competition. The five winning members at the county level would demonstrate cake-making at the State Fair. The prizes included a free trip to the fair and cash prizes of $25, $10, and $5 for the five top winners. Ena couldn't wait for next year's competition. Unfortunately, her dreams would remain unfulfilled. She would move far away from Little Falls the following year and likely never participate in another baking competition!

~~~~~~

There isn't much I remember about my first year of school living with my grandmother, Delphine, except for the bread days. Once a week, she would welcome me after school with a piece of homemade bread. When she opened the door, the baked bread aroma would envelop me like an oversized eiderdown comforter. She knew I was partial to the heel. It was wonderful: the golden crusty, chewy end piece of the loaf, warm out of the oven and smothered in butter that filled all the little nooks and crannies. It always made me feel loved and cared for.

Since Arthur had passed away, Delphine and the kids were struggling financially and barely coping. One day an unexpected guest knocked at their door. Ena answered, discovering her godfather, Eugene Heroux standing there with a friend. They had not seen Eugene for many years.

"Hello, Aunt Delphine," Eugene greeted her. "This is my good friend, Arthur St. Hilaire," introducing the stranger he had brought with him.

Eugene Heroux had married Delphine's niece Marie Anne Richard, daughter of Virginie Richard (Como), but the marriage had only lasted three years. Marie Anne had died from uremia, a fatal disease that caused her kidneys to fail. Eugene had remarried, moved to Saskatchewan, and farmed in the Bonne Madone area where Arthur St. Hilaire was homesteading.

My grandmother was confused by his unexpected visit. Eugene had not communicated with her for many years, and this visit was unannounced. Why had he brought this man named Arthur with him? What could they possibly want? She was polite and asked them to come in.

After some small talk and reminiscing about other acquaintances they both knew, Arthur finally blurted out why they had come.

"Delphine, you had a husband named Arthur; my name is Arthur. You have five children; I have five children. I believe we're destined to be together."

And the next thing that came out of Arthur's mouth was, "Delphine, will you marry me? I am leaving for

Saskatchewan in four days. I will need your answer before I leave!"

And that was the marriage proposal. Delphine had four days to decide what she and her children's fate would be for the rest of their lives. It was an anxiety-inducing, gut-wrenching, stomach-churning afternoon. Like being on a terrifying fairground ride, she wanted to vomit. All night long, all day long, her thoughts went back and forth like a metronome: to uproot them from their home, where they seemed so content and happy, or on the other hand, give them a new life with a father, someone who could provide for them. She knew how much they loved Little Falls, their friends, their cousins, and their school. This was their home, the only place they had ever known. For four agonizing days, she stewed over her decision. She could not bring herself to tell the children about the proposal.

Chapter 25

Garonne, District of Saskatchewan – 1894

In the late 1800s, the District of Saskatchewan was just starting to settle, and there were still multiple parcels of land unowned, uncleared, and uncultivated. But the word of fertile and abundant lands advertised in the Northern US states, Quebec and Europe spread quickly. Land acquisitions through the Homestead Act became immensely popular overnight and by the time Saskatchewan became a Province in 1905, 250,000 people called it home. In an 1893 Report from the Department of the Interior for the Dominion Lands of Canada, John McTaggart, the Dominion Lands and Immigration Agent for the district of Prince Albert, documents the following:

No. 16.
REPORT OF THE PRINCE ALBERT AGENT
(Mr. John McTaggart)
Prince Albert, Sask., 3rd November 1893
A.M. BURGESS, Esq.,
Deputy Minister of the Interior,
Ottawa,

SIR, - The direction that settlement had taken during the year is about the same as last year. Shell River and Stoney Creek, for the English-speaking population; St. Louis de Langevin and Duck Lake for the French are the favourite places for the newcomers. The condition of the settlers is most excellent, and this year's crop has been exceedingly abundant, the grain being everywhere of the first quality.

The only colony we have in this district is that of the Mennonites. They are steadily coming from Manitoba, others directly from Russia. They occupy a stretch of country lying south of Duck Lake, between the Saskatchewan Rivers in Townships 40 to 44, in Rages 2 to 5 west of the 3rd Meridian.

It is said that they are very prosperous, the people of the neighboring settlements doing a good business with them.

According to the entries, I should say that they number not less than 200 persons.

I have the honor to be, sir,
Your obedient servant,
JOHN McTAGGART,
Dominion Lands Immigration Agent[17]

Agents visiting settlers throughout the area during that year describe them as content with excellent crops, in fact better could scarcely be wished for and notwithstanding the usually late spring the crops all matured with rare exceptions and were all harvested before the fall frost came. They reported yields of wheat from 30 to 45 bushels per acre, slightly better for barley from 45 to 60, and oats, a massive crop was yielding all the way from 60 to 100 bushels, in many instances over 100 bushels per acre. One reported a stalk of hemp measuring fourteen and a half feet tall. Another agent made this comment:

'With an A1 soil, a bountiful supply of excellent water, abundance of coal, wood and hay to be always within easy reach of any settler, these parts of our territories have become famous and our "Cousins from over the border" have not been slow in "catching on" to these facts and are settling there in considerable numbers.'[18]

There were delegates from around the globe invited to visit the western territories, guided by a Canadian Government Land official. The free farms of one hundred-sixty acres were extremely appealing to the delegates who could view and experience the beauty and bounty with their own eyes. On August 4, 1893, a group of thirty Michigan delegates described their visit:

'The visits to these several farms proved without a doubt that the reports from that district are not exaggerated, for we found by measurements made at the experimental farm two-rowed barley, four feet high; six-rowed barley, four feet, two inches high; No. 1 Fife wheat, four feet high; rhubarb leaves, four and one-half feet in width, the stalk nine inches in circumference and twenty-two inches in length and all other products in proportion. Just before leaving this place, we visited one of the large elevators, where we found two-thousand bushels of wheat just received for shipment, brought in at 52 cents per bushel.

...

Twenty-two of the delegates took up claims for themselves and as many more were taken for friends at home.[19]

Accolades as such were not uncommon. The year prior, in August of 1892, delegates from Vermont, Maine, New Hampshire and Rhode Island visited the Prince Albert area and reported similar experiences:

'I will only say that I saw the best wheat, oats barley, potatoes cattle and land that I have ever seen. I think it is the place for a poor man.

...

Prince Albert district, one of the finest, if not the best of north west Canada. My expectations were fully satisfied. Here the climate is delightful, and the vast fields stretching far away to the horizon with a soil from two to four feet of black loam must eventually become one of the best grain and stock raising countries of the North-west.

...

The wheat, barley and oats are the best I ever saw and the potatoes are also good and the cattle simply excellent. It is the best place for a poor man to make a home for his children.

...

This great agricultural district will yet furnish comfortable homes for thousands in the future, where we see large herds of fine, fat cattle and miles of wheat, barley and oats to which this soil and climate are particularly favorable.

...

I can truthfully state that Prince Albert, Carrot River and Stoney Creek are the finest places for farming that I ever saw, well-watered and timbered, with rich soil that is practically inexhaustible, and in my opinion, there is no other place where a man can provide himself with a good home as easy. In proof of the above, I have taken land and expect to make my future home there.

...

I cannot close this report without making mention of a farmer at Duck Lake, in the Prince Albert district, who had a herd of highland cattle, some six hundred in number that are not only good, but something magnificent.'[20]

The federal government also introduced the concept of block settlement by ethnic groups. This was to ease the new homesteaders from Europe into a new country and a new culture. It allowed entire communities to leave their ancestral homes and settle in large numbers where entire townships were set aside for them. This was a successful endeavour by the government, and it attracted Mennonites from the Russian Ukraine, French immigrants, as well as Scandinavians, Icelanders, Danes, Mormons, and Doukhobors. For those struggling to survive and provide for their families in their own country, this would have been difficult to resist. Hundreds of thousands of settlers from all parts of the world poured into the region and in all, more than 625,000 land patents were issued to homesteaders.

French immigrants arriving after the 1885 Rebellion formed one of the largest French settlements in the prairies, in the St.-Louis area, which included the communities of Garonne, St-Isidore-de-Bellevue, Hoey, and Domremy. Most came from Quebec, France, and Belgium. Amongst the many Quebecers who came west were numerous Acadian exiles who had first resettled in Quebec, then resettled a second time in Minnesota, Wisconsin, and North Dakota, and were now contemplating making Saskatchewan their new home.

Many publications offering advice were available to newcomers. Two well-developed guides, Plain Facts from Farmers in Canadian North-West and Practical Hints from farmers in the Canadian North-West, were available. Both contained useful hints, and information on settling in this country, including testimonies from settlers. The guide also detailed the regulations for homesteading and land, along with proposed costs for farming. In one of its pamphlets, a settler had remarked:

'[The prairie west is] as good a place as a man can find

if he has plenty of money and brains, or if he has no money but muscle and pluck.'[21]

The French Catholic clergy also played a vital role in recruiting immigrants. Bishop Pascal of the Diocese of Prince Albert had been sent to France on a mission to find farmers. His goal was to increase the population of his diocese with Catholics. As a result, eighty-five French families had been enticed to move.

The Guigon family from Charquemont, Doubs, France, a region near the Jura Mountains bordering Switzerland, took Bishop Pascal's bait. In 1895, Emile Sr. and his wife Constantine, their six sons and two daughters, travelled forty-four hundred miles from France to Garonne, District of Saskatchewan. They settled near Little Crooked Lake. Four boys, Henri, Paul, Hyppolite, and Leon along with their father were granted homesteads of prime land. Two sons, Justin and Emile, passed away shortly after arriving in Canada.

Emilie Zoe Guigon, the eldest daughter, was my mother. She was a strong, determined woman who wanted nothing more than to be independent. At an early age, she preferred fieldwork over housework. In France, Emilie and her sister, Cecile, had become accomplished seamstresses and trained equestrians. While Cecile had difficulty adapting to Canadian prairie life, Emilie found joy in tending to the horses, gardening, or helping her father and brothers seed and harvest. She yearned for her own land, but the Dominion Lands Act would not allow it.

The 1872 Dominion Lands Act set out the conditions under which the head of a family or a single male, twenty-one years or older, would be eligible for a free quarter-section homestead grant. Until 1889, homesteaders could also "pre-empt" - that is, purchase an adjacent quarter-section homestead at a guaranteed low price when they received title to their free grant. Women could only receive a homestead if they could prove that their status as head of the household was as a widow, a divorcee, or an abandoned wife with family to support. The Homestead Land Act became open to single women when the lands of the Canadian Prairie were transferred from Federal Government to Provincial jurisdiction in 1930.

Emilie envied her brothers. She complained year after year that she wished to be self-sufficient and independent. As luck would have it, she came across a parcel of land for sale nearby.

"*Bon, Emile,*" she pleaded to her brother, Emile Jr. "There is a quarter section of land for sale from a Mr. Frank Johnson from Chicago. It is only two miles from your place and a quarter of a mile north of Hyppolite's place. The price is $3000. I have the money, and I want it!"

She would not take no for an answer.

Johnson had purchased the land from the Saskatchewan Valley Land Co. in August of 1908 for nine hundred dollars and held it for ten years before putting it up for sale.

After more coaxing and pleading, her brother Emile Jr. finally bought this quarter section and sold it to her the very same day, for the very same price. What joy. It was 1918. She was 34 years old and proudly owned a parcel of land: the NW1/4-27-44-27-W2nd. It had been partly broken and was ideally located near several Guigon homesteads. Emilie was confident she could have a crop seeded in record time. Quite an accomplishment for a female at that time.

In 1983, surveyor Mr. Belanger travelled from Ottawa to Saskatchewan to perform corrections on previously surveyed parcels. The Dominion Land Surveys for the Districts of MacKenzie, Athabasca, Saskatchewan, and Assiniboia (currently the provinces of Alberta and Saskatchewan) began in 1871. A standardized grid system consisting of meridians, townships and ranges and other lines of latitude such as baselines and correction lines were created. One township by one range was comprised of an almost perfect thirty-six square mile parcel. These thirty-six sections, each more or less six hundred and forty acres, were consecutively labelled Section 1 thru 36 and were further divided into quarters, NW, NE, SW, SE.

Belanger had been assigned the renewal of survey marks around Prince Albert, which included land in township 44, range 27 west of the second meridian, the section of land Emilie was destined to farm. His report to his Superior was dated January 9, 1894 and reads (in part) as follows:

'No. 11
REPORT OF THE P. R. A. BELANGER, D.L.S
Correction and other Surveys in Prince Albert District

T Fawcett, Esq., D.T.S.
Ottawa, 9th January, 1894

Sir, - I beg to submit the following general report on my operations during the last season, while engaged on correction surveys in the district of Prince Albert, under your direction.

On the 3rd May last I left Ottawa for Prince Albert, and reached there on the next Saturday.

There I hired my party and took possession of the horses and other articles of surveyor's outfit left the year before by William Ogilvie, D.T.S., in care of J.S. Donaldson, which I had repaired and placed in good order.

On the 17th I started from Prince Albert and proceeded to my work, which I commenced on the 3rd Meridian near "One Arrow River", proceeding eastward, making corrections in every successive range, in conformity with the memorandum of corrections submitted by the Chief Inspector of Surveys.

The work I performed during the course of the season consisted in the re-survey of Townships 44, Ranges 21A and 27; Townships 45A, Range 22 and Township 49, Range 22. I also reposted Township 44, Range 21 according to your instruction and made numerous corrections to old surveys by destroying monuments, running new lines and establishing new marks in several cases.

I also destroyed part of several lines run by D.L.S. Russell on the old system, these lines creating confusion with the new system. All the above surveys apply to townships west of the 2nd Meridian.

...

Though my work consisted mostly of re-survey of land in which different surveyors have already reported, I think a general description of the features of the country I passed over would not be out of place, owing to the great change some part of this country had undergone during the last ten years by disastrous fires, drought and other causes. I will therefore describe them as follows:

Township 44, Range 27.

In this township I opened new lines and remarked all corners, making corrections wherever possible.

Several settlers are located in this township and all are doing well.

The land is rated first class: it is well adapted for all purposes.

Good poplar wood is found in quantity in the "Manatinaw Hills" or "Highest Butte" which occupies part of the southeast quarter of the township.

...

I have the honor to be, sir,
Your obedient servant,
    P.R.A. Belanger
    L. Surveyor'[22]

The Lands Act also designated Section Allotments: all even-numbered Sections were reserved for Homesteads, and odd-numbered Sections were allotted to the C.P.R.; Sections 11 and 29 were reserved for School District purposes, while Sections 8 and 26 were retained for the Hudson Bay Company. An immigrant needed only to apply, pay the fee and put in the sweat equity to satisfy the Homestead Act conditions, and he would automatically own a piece of the Canadian Northwest Territories.

Chapter 26

Harry

I am not sure whether Mr. Belanger, the surveyor, was making corrections to the previously surveyed land because of errors or if he was actually adding correction lines to the grid. What is a correction line you ask? Every farmer knows that when the road you are driving on suddenly takes a sharp ninety-degree turn in another direction, you've encountered a correction line. If you weren't from the prairies you'd be wondering: why does the road veer off in another direction all of a sudden when there is nothing there? When there is nothing to go around? When there is no lake, no dugout or slough? Well, it's a correction line, a jog in the road that occurs every twenty-four miles to maintain a uniform six-mile by six-mile grid in the DSL system. Because of the shape of the province and the shape of the earth, uniformity could not be maintained: the latitudes would converge as you go north, eventually coming together at the North Pole.

The term is commonly used while giving directions to a farmyard. For example, this is how I might instruct my wife to find me in a field that she wasn't familiar with:

"Go three miles north, then turn left at the correction line and then continue north for another six miles until you see a green two-storey house. We are in the next field."

These were very typical directions and were easy to understand. However, my wife always had difficulty finding the correct field. She could follow directions, and she understood what a correction line was. The problem was that I was colour-blind. I could not differentiate between dark shades of brown, green, blue, and black; they were all green to me. So with six children in tow and a hot meal quickly going cold, she was never impressed with my directions; they usually led her on a wild goose chase, looking for a green house that did not exist!

I am still stuck in the imperial system; I think in miles, acres, feet, yards, pounds, and of course, bushels. It's what we grew up learning in school, and by the time metrication came to Canada in the early 1970s, most middle-aged farmers like myself struggled with the new system and were not very quick to adapt and embrace the change. After all, the construction industry remained mostly imperial. And our grid system of roads and lands surveyed designed before the turn of the twentieth century remained to this day, etched in one-mile by one-mile section. My poor mother must have found it difficult to transition from

France, a country whose system had always been metric, into Canada, a country whose system was imperial.

Chapter 27

Hoey, Saskatchewan - 1911

Over the winter of 1911-1912, Emilie and her sister Cecile accompanied their parents on a trip back to France. Other than reuniting with relatives after being away from their homeland for over fifteen years, the goal was to try and ameliorate Cecile's deep state of depression. Also, France could offer them a chance to meet some eligible bachelors. There were very few suitable unmarried men in Hoey for them, and the two sisters, aged twenty-five and twenty-eight years old were now considered old maids.

Visiting with the numerous Guigon and Fleury cousins improved Cecile's melancholy and her disposition. The sisters enjoyed their trip so much that the two women contemplated staying in France permanently. But Europe was in a period of constant upheaval, and it was evident that the declaration of war was imminent. After spending the winter abroad and being unsuccessful at securing future husbands, the two sisters returned to Canada. Cecile's depression returned and she died in 1920.

Of the eight Guigon children who travelled to start a new life in Canada, only three remained by 1925 and established families. Henri married Elimina Letarte, and they had one adopted son. Hyppolite married Marie Anna Pagnier, and they had seven daughters and two sons. Emilie married Harry Comeau Sr., and they had two sons. By the early 1920s, the three siblings were farming several quarter sections near the town of Hoey and near Little Crooked Lake. They formed a great team for seeding and harvesting. Farming was a family affair; they shared the work, the equipment, and the harvest.

Emilie continued to live with her brother Hyppolite even after she had secured her own quarter section of land. As Hyppolite's family grew, he built himself a large two-story house. His mother, Constantine, came to live with him and Emilie, once their father, Emile Sr., had passed away. The three women, Emilie, Constantine, and Marie-Anna, Hyppolite's wife, all worked together harmoniously to get the daily chores completed, cook, and raise the children.

Emilie was happy to have a lot of family nearby. She enjoyed visits from her nieces when she was tending to her own land. Most often, they would find her working in her huge garden, donning a large straw hat to keep the beating sun off her head. She had a bountiful garden, overflowing with every kind of vegetable, fruit trees, and berry bushes. Caring for her melons gave her the greatest joy, and she spent many hours nurturing them to ensure maximum sweetness and juiciness. For this endeavor, she was well-known in the community.

As was the case for most French families in the area, the Guigons were dedicated to the church and rarely missed attending Sunday service in the nearby town of St. Louis. My mother made her first Communion in St. Louis de Langevin Church (St. Louis, Sask), where she received a missal from the officiating priest, Father Xavier Barbier. It became her most treasured possession, used so much that the cover became very worn over the years. It was held together by just a few threads at the spine. She painstakingly re-stitched and re-glued the spine and affectionately recovered it with a soft dark blue velvet fabric.

Father Barbier's inscription on the first page read:

Ma chere enfant: A votre premiere communion, vous avez compris combien le bon Dieu vous a aime dans la Ste. Eucharistie, mais ce n'est qu'au Ciel que vous le comprenderez parfaitement. Payez le donc en retours, aimez-le vous aussi, soyez sans crainte et bien confiante envers lui. Recevez le frequemment. D'avoir bonnes et frequentes communion, le ciel vous est assure. X. Barbier

Translation: My dear child: In your first communion, you have understood how much God loves you through the Holy Eucharist, but only in heaven will you understand it fully. Return his love, be without fear, and have confidence in him. Receive him often. Have communion frequently, and you will be guaranteed a place in heaven.

Although she had only four years of formal schooling in France, my mother enjoyed reading and continued to educate herself. Her written French needed very little correcting. Each week she waited patiently for the delivery of *Le Patriote de L'Ouest*, a French newspaper providing communications between the French-language communities. It was published in Duck Lake.

Chapter 28

Bellevue, Saskatchewan - 1920

Like the abundant logging job opportunities advertised in the newspapers that enticed so many Quebecers to relocate to Minnesota, the promise of cheap farmland in the Saskatchewan valley had for a second time lured many Quebecers from Minnesota to the prairies. The grass always looked greener on the other side. An advertisement promised the following:

> 'Two Million Acres of the best Wheat and Flax Land
> No Floods, No Cyclones, No Droughts, No Crop Failures
> These Districts will Raise this Year Over 100 Million Bushels of Wheat
> A Golden Opportunity for the Farmer and the investor
> Over 100,000 Settlers will go into this Section this Season

You can select your own lands
The Most Marvelous Agricultural Country in the World
Your Choice of Over 200,000 Acres at $7 per Acre
The Saskatchewan Valley and Manitoba Land Company, Limited'[23]

In the late 1800s, immigration was being promoted by the Dominion of Canada, the Railway Companies, and the Colonization Companies. Almost overnight, more than thirty-five colonization companies popped up in Western Canada. The Saskatchewan Valley Land Co., formed in 1902 and based in St. Paul, Minnesota, was one of them. It had purchased over one million acres of land and had over three thousand agents working in the field to promote the glorious Saskatchewan farmland.

With ads that often overpromised, it wasn't difficult to understand why many had come, and Arthur St. Hilaire was no exception. In 1908 he moved with his wife from Minnesota to settle on farmland near Bonne Madone, Sask. His five children had been born in Saskatchewan. His two brothers, Alcide, a twin, and Wilfred, had joined him.

When Arthur's wife died in 1919, his good friend Eugene Heroux suggested that he contact his Aunt, Delphine Como, in Little Falls. Immediately he embarked on a mission to find Delphine and proposed to her.

The marriage license was issued and on March 02, 1920, the wedding took place. The following wedding article appeared in the Little Falls Herald:

'Arthur St. Hilaire of Prince Albert, Can., and Mrs. Delphine Como of Little Falls were united in marriage at St. Francis Xavier church Tuesday morning at 8 o'clock, Father Lamothe performing the ceremony. Mr. and Mrs. Frank Dufort were their attendants. Following the ceremony, a wedding dinner was served at the Dufort home.

Mrs. St. Hilaire has lived in Little Falls for seventeen years and is well known here. Mr. St. Hilaire lived here for several years, going to Canada about sixteen years ago. He owns a farm near Prince Albert. The couple left Tuesday afternoon for the twin cities to spend a week visiting relatives, after which they will go to Prince Albert.'[24]

Delphine had made her decision. She packed up her five children and their few belongings and moved to Saskatchewan. Together the Como / St. Hilaire family resettled in Bellevue. It was a small French-speaking hamlet located in the heart of the prairies. It was officially named Saint-Isidore-de-Bellevue because Saint-Isidore was widely venerated as the patron saint of farmers, peasants, labourers, and agriculture in general. Just a mile away from their new home was Manatinaw Hill, on the Minichinas range. From the top of the hill, at one thousand, eight hundred and ninety-three feet above sea level, they could see the most beautiful view of the area: the surrounding farmland, hills, Little Crooked Lake, and the town of Hoey and Bellevue; a belle view indeed!

Arthur and Delphine's marriage was one of convenience. Delphine needed financial support, and Arthur needed a mother for his five children. She was forty-four years old, starting a new life with a husband she did not know, five additional children to care for, and a very foreign environment. She was comfortable in Little Falls, where the population had swelled to over five thousand people, where she had family close by and neighbours right next door. She was accustomed to strolling downtown into the St. Paul Store, Victor Clothing Company or Burton Stores where an assortment of plain and fancy dresses, spring coats in wool and other weaves and patent leather shoes with buttons and lace were sold. There were millinery shops, carrying dress fabrics, lace silk hosiery, and the latest styles in hats to try on to your heart's content. And there was her favourite store: J.C. Penny.

Overnight she had become a farmer's wife in a new landscape, with no one around for miles. Her home was now a rural parcel of land, identifiable not by a street name and a house number but only by the DLS grid system: Section 18, Township 44, Range 27, West of the Second Meridian.

My poor grandmother!! The closest urban center was Prince Albert, forty miles away.

Overnight her family had grown to include ten children aged four to seventeen. They were now living in cramped conditions, a very small house which made their apartment above the saloon in Little Falls seem like a Grand Hotel! The only world her children had ever known no longer existed. They had a new father, five new siblings to share life with, farm work, and a country school. They were instantly immersed in an almost completely French-speaking community. But their worst hardship was losing their identities as Comos; overnight, they became Comeaus. Bellevue was a very French community and the name Comeau, the original spelling, was better suited for this region. Of the four schools in the immediate area, Bellevue School, Gaudet School, Ethier School, and Argonne School, the younger Comeau children resumed their education at Bellevue School with the St. Hilaire children. The older boys Harry, 17, and Norman, 15, set out to work as hired hands.

The children and Delphine soon adapted to their environment. They quickly became involved in community activities, many of which revolved around the church. Five years after arriving in Bellevue, a new priest, Father Bernard, was selected to guide the congregation of Bellevue. The area was expanding quite rapidly, and with the Roman Catholic population swelling to over four hundred souls, a new church had to be built. The current church, a repurposed schoolhouse, could no longer accommodate this fast-growing community. The question of where to build the new church divided the community into three! Lines had been drawn creating dissension amongst the congregation. And once a decision had been made, it fueled even greater conflict among the discontented parishioners. Some unhappy families moved to Batoche or Domremy.

Nonetheless, a decision had been made, and money had to be raised. A large Bazaar was organized in the community to raise funds. Two candidates, Ena Comeau and Bernadette Gaudet were elected to drive the fundraising efforts. When Ena discovered that the first event would be a bake-off, she was ecstatic. Her competitive spirit had never waned after her bread-baking days in Little Falls. Soliciting the help of her mother, Ena baked a fabulous three-layer chocolate cake that brought in $32, while Bernadette's cake sold for $15. Ena was confident that she would pull in the most funds for the fundraiser. Next, the two young ladies would each organize a soiree at their respective homes. Approximately $130 was raised at the St. Hilaire house, while $71 was raised at Mr. Emery Gaudet's house.

The Bazaar organizing committee was also busy developing the itinerary for the two-day event scheduled for November 25 and 26. Along with items donated for sale, there would be a Wheel of Fortune, *Peches Miraculeuse*, a fishing game, and two comedy acts: *Georgette Est Si Nervous* (Georgette is so nervous), played by the women and *Le Cambrioleur Malgre Lui*, (The Reluctant Robber), performed by the men. A more serious play named *Le Poignard* (The Dagger) would also be performed on one of the two nights along with the musical choir of Bellevue school.

The bazaar results were tallied, and a total of $2223 was raised. Together, Ena and Bernadette had brought in more than half of all proceeds. Baskets, sewn from floral fabrics and adorned with ribbons and laces, were auctioned off for $300. This had been another endeavour by the two young ladies. With an endless treasure trove of remnants from her Mother's sewing bin, Ena spent hours embellishing her baskets, and it paid off. It had been a great effort by both candidates. When all was said and done, Ena's final total of $531 was just shy of beating Bernadette's total of $580. These two young ladies were exemplary role models in their community. The organizing committee was thrilled with the results.

The crowds enjoyed the games, and the plays received rave reviews. *Le Cambioleur Malgre Lui*, whose main character Popette was played by Norman Comeau, received the most accolades! Norman also portrayed the first guard in the tragedy *Le Poignard*. He had discovered his passion for acting since coming to Bellevue and began volunteering for the leading roles in many of the community's theatrical plays at the parish hall. Typically, Elimina Guigon, Henri Guigon's wife, took charge of the musical numbers and directed the plays. She was an extremely talented lady; her performances always guaranteed a hall packed to the rafters, and comments of *"on n'a rit pour son argent"* (we got a good laugh for our money) could be heard as people left the hall. The organizing committee thanked all the parishioners for their participation and generosity. The finale was always a chorus of *"y'en a pas comme nous"* which everyone joined in.

The contract for the construction of the church and Presbytery was awarded to Mr. H. Baribeau of Domremy. By May 1926, the work had already begun, and by the end of August, the benediction after laying the first brick was celebrated. *Le Patriot de l'Ouest* reported a crowd of five to six hundred people in attendance from surrounding areas of Duck Lake, Rosthern Carlton, Batoche, Wakaw, Bonne Madame, Domremy, Hoey, St. Louis, Crystal

Springs, and Prince Albert. The Guigons, the St. Hilaire's, and the Comeaus were in attendance and all decked out in their Sunday best. The women with cloche hats dresses sewn from fancy goods, of crepe, satin, or voile, embroidered and trimmed in lace; the men in their regular dark suits, a few in light summer suits with neckties and hats of all sorts, their hair slicked back and neatly tucked under a boater, flat cap or fedora hat. Between one hundred and twenty-five and one hundred and fifty cars were parked around the church and along the road. After the ceremony, the crowd moved to the Church basement for refreshments. There was standing room only.

Norman and his younger brother Clarence were amongst the many community members to be recruited to work on the new church. Having little education and without receiving any formal instruction, Norman wired the church and rectory ready for electricity.

It was well known in the community that the Comeau children had a reputation for being self-starters, capable of tackling any job, large or small, whether they had observed someone doing it beforehand or not. That's just the way their minds worked. And they had a strong work ethic and would stop at nothing to get the job done quickly and perfectly. One could say they worked like dogs or kept their nose to the grindstone. These traits were very typical of most Saskatchewan pioneers; they possessed a strong work ethic, a jack-of-all-trades skillset, and the ability to MacGyver anything.

~~~~~~

I considered myself a jack-of-all-trades, a MacGyver, so to speak. Like most farmers, I learned to troubleshoot and repair everything without instruction. I taught myself wiring, plumbing, welding, mechanical, roofing, and building renovations just by observing how things worked or how they were put together. I configured ways to fix or patch things. The resulting fix wasn't always the prettiest or neatest, but damn it, it usually worked!

In the nineteen sixties, Comeau Construction built many roads in the area, including the Birch Hills road and the Bellevue road. The Bellevue road started at the junction of the town of Domremy and highway #2. It ran west to Bellevue, circling Manatinaw Hill. This hill, a mere four miles south of our home, became a ski resort in the mid-sixties, named Minitinas. It was practically in our back yard! The year it opened, I bought myself and my three oldest girls skis for Christmas. We enjoyed many hours of skiing on that hill.

Clarence was no exception to hard work. Tasked with moving all of the graves from the old Bellevue site to the new cemetery site located behind the church was a daunting job for a seventeen-year-old boy. One by one, he dug up the graves, carefully removed the remains, and carted them to the new graves, which he also had to dig. Like his grandfather, Elzear, who was digging graves half a century before him, Clarence worked tirelessly until the job was done.

While the church was being built, Father Bernard arranged for his two nieces, Oliva and Aline, to travel from Quebec to help him out. The two sisters came to assist him with the household duties and cooking his meals. During this time, Norman met Oliva, and after a brief courtship, they married.

The rectory was completed on November 8th, 1926, and by December 25th, the church was ready to welcome the congregation for Christmas mass. By 1927 the Bellevue parish was firmly established, and the hamlet and surrounding area began to thrive as more francophones moved into the region from France, Quebec, and the US. Around this time, the Garonne Post Office amalgamated with the Bellevue Post Office, and the area known as Garonne disappeared from the map of Saskatchewan.

Chapter 29

Hoey, Saskatchewan - 1920

In 1901 Saskatchewan had 13,445 active farms, covering 600,000 acres; by 1911, the province had 95,013 farms covering 9.1 million acres; by 1916, 14 million acres had been cultivated, mainly in wheat. Grain farming was the backbone of the prairie economy and its way of life. Built out of necessity and efficiency, grain elevators began to dominate the Saskatchewan skyline in the early 1900s. They became the lifeblood of every small prairie community and an iconic symbol of prosperity.

Emilie Guigon's quarter section was geographically located between several French parishes, all within a ten-mile radius: Hoey, St. Louis, Saint-Isidore-de-Bellevue, and Domremy. It was the most convenient location. So many towns close by provided numerous opportunities: the choice of where to attend church, where to buy supplies and groceries, and the advantage of belonging to several communities for activities. Whether it was a fall supper, a wedding reception, or a curling bonspiel, the family felt welcomed at these community centers and often attended many functions. In addition, within reach were two larger centres: Duck Lake, forty miles to the west via the St-Laurent Grandin Ferry, and the city of Prince Albert, thirty miles to the north.

The town of Hoey was the closest, situated about four and a half miles northeast of Emilie's homestead. The Grand Trunk Railway, built in 1914, hugged the east edge of town, where four grain elevators proudly displayed the name HOEY in giant block letters.

In the 1920s, it was one of the most thriving and prosperous commercial centres in the area; it boasted a bank, a hotel, two general stores, a town hall, a central telephone exchange, a hardware store, a lumberyard, a couple of agricultural implement dealerships, a blacksmith shop, a gas station, an auto mechanic garage, a foundry, a shoemaker and a resident doctor. The large town hall built by the townspeople could easily accommodate about sixty families. It was the cultural hub of the community and also served as a chapel for Sunday mass. It put an end to the weekly trek to St. Louis to attend church, a welcoming change for the Hoey parishioners.

The surrounding farmland in the grain belt was so named for its strip of rich fertile soil. It had not been a lie or an exaggeration by earlier recorded reports of delegates visiting the area. It was indeed good black loam with clay subsoil, excellent for mixed crop farming, and often yielded bumper crops. By 1918, the farmland around Hoey was completely bought out. People had heard that once you drank the water from Saskatchewan, you couldn't stop drinking it. It was the pull of the land, the lifestyle, and the opportunities. It was addictive, and people quickly swarmed the prairies, hoping to cash in on the wealth. Within another ten years, the urban population of Hoey had grown to one hundred and fifty people; the rural population had grown to fifteen thousand.

During this time the Saskatchewan School Trustees' Association had called for English-only instruction in schools. The locals in this predominantly francophone area were determined to retain their French language and culture. The government obliged by amending the School Act, which allowed French instruction for first graders only and one hour per day for all other grades; the last half hour of school was dedicated to catechism.

An organization in Quebec called *Societe du Parler Francais* du Canada invited francophones of Saskatchewan to select delegates to attend their major convention the following year. *Le Patriot de l'Ouest* newspaper published an article recruiting French Catholics to become ambassadors for their districts and to attend a meeting in Duck Lake.

In the St.-Louis/Hoey area, the Guigons volunteered. Emilie, her sister Cecile and her brothers Hyppolite, Henri, and Emile, along with four hundred and fifty francophones, met in Duck Lake, and a provincial chapter was formed. Shortly after, the society was renamed A.C.F.C. (*L'Association Catholique Franco-Canadienne*).

A.C.F.C. was founded to bring together French Canadians and promote, protect and defend their language, religion, and culture: *la vrai foi, la belle langue* (the true faith, the beautiful language). In 1925, A.C.F.C. delegates proposed that French examinations be organized and administered to participating A.C.F.C. chapters throughout the province. The *concours* (competition) would engage the teachers and students and help them improve their French language skills. The examination would occur annually, in June. Book awards would be given to the students with top marks in grammar, composition, and spelling. What better way to stimulate the kids than a friendly competition?

On June 20, 1925, the first *concours* took place with eighty schools registered and one thousand and sixty-two participants from across the province. It was an overwhelming success, surpassing the A.C.F.C. delegate's expectations. The St-Louis/Hoey chapter was a very active group, thirty members strong. They submitted thirteen schools and one convent for participation.

In preparation for the upcoming annual regional A.C.F.C. convention and award ceremonies, the town of Hoey was a busy hub of activity. More than a dozen persons volunteered to decorate the town. Banners were hung, and wooden platforms were built for the outdoor banquet and presenting the awards. More than five hundred people attended.

The following year, the province registered thirteen hundred and sixty-three students across 103 schools. Over three hundred and fifty prizes were awarded. The St-Louis/Hoey district ceremony took place in Domremy and attracted more than two thousand people. Honour students received book awards, and top mark recipients were given a gold or silver medal engraved with the words: St-Louis/Hoey and their grade number. Whichever community hosted these events, the Guigon family always attended. The French language was very important to them.

Chapter 30

Harry

When my mother, Emilie Guigon, immigrated from France to Saskatchewan in the late 1800s, she brought with her a very polished Parisian French language. Her written word was also impeccable. I vividly remember my mother's Petit Larousse Illustre, an early 1920s edition French dictionary. It was one of her most prized possessions, only second to her bible.

The francophone population in our community was comprised of many Acadian exiles who had fled to Quebec and later resettled in Saskatchewan. Like the Comeaus, their roots date back to the seventeenth century, and many had maintained their Acadian culture and heritage. Similar to the Chiac or Brayon dialects of New Brunswick, our language was developed from our Acadian and French roots and greatly influenced by English.

Phrases like: *Y' mouille* (it's raining), *Y' m'engage* (he hired me), *Barrer la porte* (lock the door), *Y'a cassé la loi* (he broke the law), were understood by everyone. We utilized words such as *char* (car), *marabout* (grumpy), *bibitte* (beetle), *catin* (doll) and *badrer* (bother). Except for *bibitte* and *badrer*, all these words could be found in Mother's Larousse dictionary, but they did not have the meaning we thought they did. For instance, *char* means a cart, a float (as in a parade) or a tank (military); and *marabout* means a type of African witch doctor, a tent, or a bird. The word *catin*, what little girls called their dolls, was also commonly used as a term of endearment by everyone: you are a "doll" (*catin*). To my astonishment, Mother's dictionary defined *catin* as a whore, prostitute, or a woman of bad morals!

English words such as vacuum, tires, sweater, and bumper crop, to name a few, were inserted spontaneously into our everyday French language. We shifted effortlessly from one language to another, all in the same sentence, and everyone understood. English verbs were conjugated in French modes all over the place, and it flowed together naturally.

Franglais, half French, half English… *ce moment when you start penser en deux langues at the same temps* (the moment you start thinking in two languages at the same time)!

After my first year of school at Bellevue School, I attended Argonne School. It was a one-room country school about two-and-one-half miles from home. There are memories from those years at Argonne School that have never left me. I travelled there with my brother, Andy, and my Guigon cousins by buggy in the summer and by cutter in the winter. It was a new school, built in 1935, with a big cast-iron box stove where those who sat near it roasted and those who sat further away froze.

As early as 1911, the provincial government had decided to assimilate the francophone minority into the anglophone majority and began limiting French language education to one hour per day. By 1931 they had banned French instruction completely, and laws were passed that made English the only permissible language. French was even forbidden at recess. So, while we learned English at school, our mother tongue remained French outside of school. I remember many of my teachers throughout the years who could not speak a word of French and others who could not speak a word of English. It was impossible to obtain a good education, and it is not surprising we spoke a mixture of the two languages. My education ended before the end of eighth grade. That year I attended only fifty days.

I also remember the *Examens de Francais*, the obligatory yearly exams we took. The exams consisted of three parts: grammar, composition, and spelling/reading, each lasting one hour long. They were always scheduled on a Saturday morning in June. What young boy wanted to be sitting in a hot, stuffy classroom for three hours on a Saturday morning in the nicest month of the year? Not me! And the results were posted in *Le Patriot de l'Ouest* newspaper, to boot. I don't recall ever being excited about taking part in these exams; it did not make me jump for joy or hoot and holler!

The newspaper listed every participant's name, their school, their town, and their score. There were two categories of schools: A-schools had more than two classrooms, and B-schools had two or fewer classrooms.

One-room schools had the greatest challenge: one teacher, multiple grades, and only one hour of French instruction allowed per day. Argonne was designated as a B school.

For those students who struggled in school, the exam was gruelling, a test of endurance. And then seeing their low scores posted beside their names in the paper, well, that did nothing to encourage them or boost their confidence for next year's competition. Thankfully, in later years only grades over seventy, *promus avec honneur* (promoted with honour), were posted beside the student's name. Those who received grades lower than seventy, but a passing grade over fifty percent, were grouped in a paragraph below, names only, no scores. Those who excelled in school and scored high marks were always eager and excited to check out their names in the newspaper and their standing, not only against their classmates, but also province-wide.

In Grade Five, I scored seventy-one percent, beating out my cousin Josie Guigon's mark of seventy percent. That was a proud moment for me.

Later, when my children were subjected to taking the same *Conours de Francais*, top achievers in each school received book awards. The kids were always so excited to get these books, however, their enthusiasm would often soon diminish. Many of these books came from France and the content was not always suitable or applicable for children in rural Saskatchewan. I remember my nine-year-old daughter, bringing me one of her newly gifted books and asking me to decipher the content. It was called "*Le Roi Tonne et le Gnome farceur*" (One Ton King and the Prankster Gnome). It contained two stories describing the metric system. The first story presented the facts on weights: tons, grams, kilograms, milligrams, micrograms etc. and the second story illustrated volume: litres, kiloliters, centilitres, etc.... It was Greek to her! And of course this system was foreign to me. I did not comprehend anything in that book. At that time our rulers and tape measures contained only feet and inches; there were no markings beneath indicating centimetres or millimetres. And we only knew of miles, not kilometres! Our scales calculated weights in ounces and pounds; our measuring containers were in cups, gallons and bushels! If my mother had still been around she would have been the ideal person to explain this system to my daughter and perhaps I could have learnt a little bit about metrication at that same time.

Chapter 31

Hoey, Saskatchewan – 1925

Harry, and his brother, Norman, came to work as hired hands on Emilie's new homestead, in the early 1920s. Her quarter section of land, which she was slowly clearing with her two brother's assistance, was not yet ready for seeding. A newly acquired section of land meant continual, laborious work. There was an immediate panic to accomplish the task as quickly as possible, because it would provide the best opportunity to obtain a return on the land as quickly, sometimes even in the same year. Harry and Norman enjoyed working for Emilie. She was a strong, industrious woman who could handle anything a man could, and she put in as many long hours as they did. They made a good team.

It wasn't long before Emilie and Harry realized that they enjoyed each other's companionship and shared similar ideas, philosophies, and goals. After a short courtship, Harry, aged 21, and Emilie, aged 40, were married. It was November 25, 1924.

For the first few years of marriage, Harry and Emilie lived on Hyppolite's homestead in a small house. Once their land had been cleared, they moved the house and chicken coop to their quarter section. The following year, Andre, their first child, was born.

They continued farming with Emilie's two brothers, Hyppolite and Henri. In August 1925, they harvested their first crop, a bumper crop, yielding fifty to sixty bushels per acre. But the weather turned cold in early October and temporarily halted the harvest. It was not uncommon for the harvest season to extend well into fall, especially when it was a high-yielding crop, which substantially increased the workload. When they finally finished in the field, they had amassed a high-quality crop, one of the largest ever.

Saskatchewan weather was always unpredictable, and each year the farmers were at the mercy of mother nature. It directly affected their livelihood. When farmers gathered at the Hoey bar for a beer, small talk always revolved around the weather. Too much rain, not enough rain, rain at the wrong time, too hot, not enough sun, too cold. Sometimes, after just one beer, the weather had changed entirely, and so had their moods.

The next few years proved to be productive for the couple and the surrounding farmers. The average Saskatchewan farm grew to over 370 acres, more than a half-section. The dry climate and short growing season were the most serious stumbling blocks for wheat production during this time.

A Dominion Experimental Farm in Indian Head, Saskatchewan, began production trials of a new early-ripening wheat, genetically selected for prairie conditions. It was a cross between Red Fife wheat and Hard Red Calcutta wheat which would mature 7-10 days earlier than their usual seeding of Red Fife wheat. This newly improved variety of wheat, named Marquis, along with the government's promotion of summer-fallowing to conserve soil moisture and control weeds, led to a robust agricultural expansion in the area. When these processes were used in conjunction with gas tractors and threshing machines, they substantially reduced labour hours. Needing fewer horses for harvest meant freeing land that had been dedicated to growing oats and hay for the animals. There were now more acres for seeding wheat and as a result, production exploded.

The Comeaus and the Guigons continued to thrive, keeping busy with their farming, animals, and gardens. Many activities in their community kept them occupied. When they got wind that a rail load of new farm implements had arrived in town, they eagerly congregated with fellow farmers to see the latest equipment. That was always exciting! They never missed a farm auction sale in the area, knowing a good bargain could be negotiated. They attended many of the demonstrations on new equipment put on by companies, like the demo on Carter Day Discs machines. It had attracted a good crowd in Hoey. In addition, they attended many community events, all of the performances put on by their local A.C.F.C. Chapter group and by other chapters from surrounding towns.

The Guigons were a very musical family and enjoyed these outings regularly.

The next two eldest Comeau siblings married within a few years of Harry and Emilie, also in November. Ena married Emilien Ethier in 1926 and made their home in Hoey. Norman married Oliva Bernard in 1928 and settled in Bellevue near Manatinaw Hill. November was an ideal time for a wedding; the harvest was complete, and the cold weather was setting in. Both siblings continued to engage in community events; Norman continued to act in community plays and regularly played checkers on the St-Jacques team in Bellevue against the rival team called the Nationals. Shortly after their marriages, both Ena and Norman began their families. Ena and Emilien had ten children; nine survived. Norman and Oliva had five children, three born in Saskatchewan and the last two born in Quebec. The move to Quebec was one that Oliva had wished for a long time.

Chapter 32

Harry

I inherited my tremendous energy and my work ethic from both my mother and my father. I've never been able to sit still. I have always enjoyed being challenged when presented with difficult tasks and demanding schedules. My hands have always been kept busy. A sprint, a scurry, a scamper, or a steady jog, would correctly describe my usual pace. Surprisingly, my appetite was poor; taking time to eat was never a priority, and I often went without a meal if I was left to my own devices. However, this lack of nourishment never impeded my strength or my hyperactiveness. I possessed immense power for a man, five-foot-six inches tall and weighing one hundred and twenty pounds. Today, I would have likely been diagnosed with ADHD!

During the 1920's and 1930s, the average marrying age

for a woman was twenty-one. So, it was likely that many had perceived my mother as a spinster, an old maid. She was forty years old, well past the average age, when she married my father.

Nothing about my mother could be construed as average. While it may be common today for a woman to capture a man half their age, in 1924, it was unprecedented. It was undoubtedly fuel to initiate small-town gossip and cause tongues to wag!

My mother also thrived as a farmer, which was an unusual occupation in those days. During this time in Canada, women farmers were frowned upon, perceived as deviant, and it was deemed acceptable only under exceptional circumstances. It was considered an occupation exclusively for males.

Nevertheless, she felt that she had the right to cultivate land just like any male and believed in her abilities to do so. The 1872 Dominion Land Act prohibited acquisition by single females. The fact that she could not apply for a homestead and be given free land like her brothers had received, likely motivated her.

She was very successful with her farming endeavours and managed to thrive even during the great depression years. She was an innovative woman with modern ideas, attitudes, and ambitions, considered radical by the standards of the time.

Chapter 33

Hoey, Saskatchewan – 1929

When the summer of 1929 arrived, my mother was overjoyed to discover she was expecting a second child. She was forty-five years old.

"Can you bring in some more firewood," Emilie asked Harry just as Edmond Delude, their hired hand, came into the house. He had just completed the night shift. The three men, Harry, Norman, and Edmond, were working around the clock to clear a half section of land near Little Crooked Lake. Harry and Emilie had just recently purchased this parcel, and their goal was to get this land ready for spring seeding. It was located one mile south and three miles east of their home quarter: SW & SE ¼ 29-44-27 W2, directly between her father Emile's and her brother Paul's original homesteads. The job was proving to be very challenging. It was overgrown with dense shrubs and bush, the thickest plot they had ever cleared.

Emilie added a few more logs to the stove and started to serve breakfast. The oats and milk that had been simmering in a saucepan for some time were now ready. Little Andy had just awoken and sat patiently at the table waiting for his porridge. They ate breakfast together. Afterward, Edmond went home to sleep, and Harry took his turn working the land.

Emilie busied herself with house cleaning, dishes, floors, and the chores that were a part of her daily routine. She couldn't wait to get out of the house and tend to her horses. She quickly bundled up little Andy and off they went to the chicken coop to collect the eggs. Finally, the best part of the day came: off to the barn to feed and groom the horses. They were her pride and joy, and she never tired of looking after them. It brought memories of her sister and their time in France participating in equine competitions. She had the soft skills and patience to be a great equestrian. So while little Andy amused himself with an old milk pail, she indulged in her favourite pastime: fetching clean water, laying fresh straw for their bedding, and brushing their coats and manes. But what she enjoyed most was the social companionship her horses provided.

Harry battled the brush on the new parcel of land. It was a difficult task, especially by himself. The bush was dense, and he could see only a few inches in front of him. He diligently swung the ax, cutting hundreds of branches jutting out in all directions, always ready to poke an eye out. It was a daunting task. But the work by hand had to be done first until the clearing was large enough to bring in the big guns. They had purchased A15-30, an

International Harvester tractor on steel wheels, which would significantly accelerate the work and reduce the manpower. Before any tilling could commence, all the large rocks and boulders had to be removed. The weather had been cooperative so far. There was still no snow to contend with, but the ground was starting to freeze up, and soon, tilling would become impossible until spring.

Their hope to seed a crop of Marquis wheat in early spring would provide the best opportunity to pay off the land free and clear within the first year. Then, once the seeding was complete, the only thing left to do was to pray for good weather. And if perfect or ideal growing conditions were not in the cards, they would pray that the crop survived drought, hail storms, grasshopper plagues, raging prairie fires, or whatever Mother Nature threw at them.

"Ah Norman, so glad to see you," Harry called out as his brother rode up on his horse. "I sure could use your help. I have been struggling with these stubborn roots all morning, and now I have another one of my darn nosebleeds. Can you take over for a while?"

Norman had stopped to assess the progress on Harry's land.

"You must have a good couple hundred acres completed. Slightly more than a hundred to go."

They were both pleased with their progress.

"Do you think we can get this finished before the winter weather sets in?" Harry asked.

"Yes, I am hopeful we can if we continue at this pace," Norman replied.

All three men were extremely hard-working, "get 'er done" type of guys. Nothing stopped them from forging ahead when faced with near-impossible tasks and schedules or even illness.

Norman jumped on the tractor and waited for Harry's instructions.

"Go ahead, back up," Harry yelled, "I need more slack on the straps."

Once the tree roots were securely strapped to the tractor, he gave the hand signal to Norman.

"Go cautiously. I don't want the leather straps to split."

Without any resistance, the tractor yanked the roots out of the ground.

Norman continued to work for various farmers, mostly for Harry and Emily, whenever they needed an extra hand. Harry appreciated his brother's work and always made sure he got paid. However, this wasn't always the case. Norman had spent the entire summer moving rocks and pulling roots for his stepfather, Arthur St. Hilaire. When the job was completed, he was handed an old pair of overalls for the work he had accomplished. *"Ces't tous! Un veille salopette avec bavette*? That's it? An old pair of overalls?" lamented Norman. He was exasperated. How was he supposed to feed his family with a pair of overalls?? Norman worked tirelessly, but money was often scarce, and like many other hired hands, he did not always receive fair compensation.

As many successes of high-yielding crops reported in the early years of homesteading, there were plenty of unreported failures. It was a demanding lifestyle. The initial cost of establishing a crop on the land, even if the land was obtained at low expense under homestead conditions, often depleted all the little money they had. Many settlers had failed attempts, disastrous results, and abandoned their farms. Hired hands were crucial to the development of the prairie farms. They worked long hours for little pay, four to five dollars a day, plus room and board. Those who were poorly treated by their employers or did not receive their payment would simply walk off the job and find another. Workers were always in demand for harvesting and helping with the animals. Most were transient immigrants who wanted to acquire some capital and the experience they needed to secure their own homestead.

By the end of October, there remained only a few acres left to clear on Emilie and Harry's newest half-section. It had been an endurance test, but their hard work would pay off the following spring. There was one last dense thicket to clear. Harry had been working the night shift and was feeling dizzy and weak when Norman showed up for the next shift.

"Go on home and rest up," Norman insisted when he noticed Harry was struggling with another nosebleed. Resting was not what Harry wanted to do. They were so close to finishing, that he did not want to stop, but he had no choice. He mounted his horse and rode home. Emilie immediately tended to him, trying to stop the bleeding.

Harry had frequent nosebleeds, but otherwise, he seemed perfectly healthy. No one knew why this occurred as often as it did, and no one questioned it. This time it was different. After a couple of days, Harry's nose was still bleeding. He had lost a lot of blood and was growing very weak. On November 2nd, Emilien Ethier, his sister Ena's husband, and Norman took Harry by sleigh to the hospital in Prince Albert, thirty miles away.

Chapter 34

Harry

For ten days, the doctors at Holy Family Hospital in Prince Albert tried everything to stop my father's nose bleed. Two operations were performed, one on November 3rd and November 5th, to cauterize the bleeding vessels in the nose. All attempts failed. My father died a long slow death on November 12, 1929, at 10:00 pm, at the age of twenty-six. J.W. Ede, his physician noted the cause of death as 'epistaxis' followed by 'emesis' and 'exhaustion'. 'Epistaxis', refers to a nosebleed, 'emesis', refers to vomiting and 'exhaustion' - well that was not surprising given the ten days of suffering he endured. The secondary contributing factor was recorded as 'always has been frail'. M.C. Hamilton was the undertaker. He was buried in the Bellevue cemetery on November 15.

Three months later, my mother delivered me at home on February 24, 1930. Father Bernard baptized me in the Bellevue rectory on March 25, 1930. My godparents were my uncle, Hippolite Guigon, and my aunt Anne-Marie Pagnier.

In 1934, my mother married a second time to Louis Favenec; she was fifty years old, and Louis was sixteen years her junior. They did not have any children. Before my mother passed away in 1958, she wrote her will stating that her husband, Louis, could have full use of her lands along with the profits until he passed away. Then, they were to be passed on to her two sons, my brother Andy and me and her two grandsons, Marc and Jacques. Since my Mother seemed to be a modern woman, ahead of her time it surprises me that she willed the land to the male grandchildren only. Four granddaughters had been born before the grandsons. But at least she didn't follow the primogeniture system of inheritance in which a person's property passes only to their firstborn legitimate child upon their death.

It was never determined if my father had an underlying medical condition to produce such massive vascular bleeding that led to his death. Was he a hemophiliac, a genetically inherited condition? As far as I know, no one in my family has inherited hemophilia! Perhaps he suffered from vascular malformations? Or maybe it was related to a tumour, trauma, a bleeding disorder, or another disease? We will never know why they could not stop the bleeding. Many deaths that occurred in previous generations are now treatable. Dying from such disorders is almost unheard of today.

While I am awaiting my second surgery for lung cancer at St. Paul's Hospital in Saskatoon, I am perplexed. I have never smoked a single cigarette or cigar in my entire life. Lung cancer is unexpected and even more so in a second occurrence. It takes you by surprise. But I believe and accept what God has chosen for me. He was kind enough to give me five wonderful years after my first surgery, so I remain optimistic. Growing up in a very strict French Catholic community I went to church every Sunday without question, without fail. My deeply ingrained Catholic convictions were set at a very early age. I knew that the faithful were obliged to participate in the Holy Eucharist on Sundays, unless excused for a serious reason and that those who deliberately failed in this obligation committed a grave sin. So my entire life, no matter where I was on earth, if it was a Sunday I went to church. My belief in God, heaven and life after death was always very, very strong; strong enough that I knew I had to live my life on earth accordingly. I am confident that, again, God will help pull me through this surgery and I will be out of here running around very soon - literally! Those who know me will attest to my stubborn streak. I am a man who refuses to let anything or anyone slow me down.

Lying in my hospital bed allows me to reflect on my life, my family, and my ancestors. I think a lot about my father and imagine what he was like. Sometimes my mind is blank. Other times I think I can picture him. But the memories are only from the stories told by my mother, aunt, or grandmother and from a handful of yellowed patinaed photographs, photos I treasure dearly.

I've always been reserved and quiet. I seldom raise my voice, and I have never been forthcoming with expressing my emotions. It seems to me that most Acadians had these characteristics. They took everything in stride, good times and bad times. They seldom displayed emotion and little complaining was ever heard from them. They were always happy. Like me. Was my father happy in life?

My ancestors were pioneers in Nova Scotia, New Brunswick, Quebec, and Saskatchewan. They were not the first people on the land, but their hands may have been the first to clear and work the virgin soil, the first to cultivate it, sow a crop, and harvest it. Like his ancestors, my father loved farming. And like my father, I also loved farming and tilling the Hoey soil. It was a connection we had with the land, the feeling of ownership, the freedom, and the accomplishment - to grow, to nurture, to savour - those were the reasons that compelled us to be farmers.

I believe I am cut from the same cloth as my ancestors. We shared similar ideas, opinions, and beliefs. It was in my genes to carry on the tradition of farming, and until the early 1990s, I devoted my days to caring for our land. I will always possess a fondness for our Saskatchewan farmland, the land of superlatives, the breadbasket of Canada. Have you ever experienced the amazing dance of a wheat field in the wind? When the wheat bends in the breeze for as far as the eye can see? The soft swaying of a golden canola field under a blue sky? Or the reflection of the sun on the periwinkle blooms of a flax field? It is nature's alchemy captured. I am often overwhelmed by the beauty of the prairies.

Whether my ancestors were fleeing from the hardships in their homeland, fleeing to escape the British, or out of necessity for survival, they were seldom intimidated by the unknown. They were ambitious, and if it meant starting over again in a foreign land to find a comfortable and peaceful life, they weren't afraid to do so.

The tragic events of the Great Upheaval still weigh heavily on my heart and my mind. The Acadians were kind, loving, and friendly people. They were willing to share their knowledge and their wealth. They wanted only to live in peace. I believe that if France had retained control of Nova Scotia in the mid-1700s and the expulsion of the Acadians had never happened, the amicable relationship between the Mi'kmaq and Acadians would have culminated into a distinct society. Perhaps a new country called Acadimaq or Mikadia, where they would have continued to live peacefully and happily together.

Much like Quebec's motto: *Je me souviens, que né sous le lys, je croîs sous la rose*, meaning, I remember, that I was born under the lily, and I grow under the rose. The lily represents France, and the Rose represents England. It reaffirms that they will always remember the origins of their ancestors, their culture and their traditions. As an Acadian, I will also never forget that: I was born under the lily (France), expelled under the Rose (England), but now thrive all over the world: under the purple violet (New Brunswick), under the lady's slipper (P.E.I.), under the Mayflower (Nova Scotia), under the western red lily (Saskatchewan), under the magnolia grandiflora (Louisiana), under the Hibiscus (Haiti), under the lily (France), under the rose (England, and the United States) and under the maple leaf (all of Canada).

Children, grandchildren, and great-grandchildren, I hope this story instills one important message in each of you: leading a life consistent with high morals, strong values, and ethical principles will be the greatest predictor of your happiness.

Acknowledgments:

I am grateful to every genealogist, historian, and Acadian descendant, who helped me fill in the gaps of my family's history. Your willingness to share information online motivated me to keep searching for the missing records and documents that helped tie this story together and create an accurate account of the events of my ancestors journey from Acadia to Saskatchewan.

To my family (daughter, mother, siblings, cousins, husband): your contribution came in many ways and each one of you had a tremendous impact on the success of this project.

To my good friend Carol Gossner: you opened my eyes to the different possibilities of making this a great story.

To my father for being the inspiration.

Merci à tous pour votre précieuse collaboration!
Thank-you everyone for your precious collaboration!

References / Sources:

1. Acadian & French-Canadian Ancestral / Lucie LeBlanc Consentino: http://www.Acadian-home.org/frames.html
2. A Great & Noble Scheme / John Mack Faragher
3. Genealogique des Familles Acadiennes / Stephen A. White / Patrice Gallant / Hector-J. Hebert
4. Genealogie des Familles Acadiennes / Placid Gaudet:http://139.103.17.56/cea/livres/doc.cfm?livre=placide
5. The Acadian Migrations / Robert A Leblanc: https://www.erudit.org/fr/revues/cgq/1967-v11-n24-cgq2598/020742ar.pdf
6. Acadians in Halifax and on Georges Island, 1755 1764 / Ronnie-Gilles Leblanc: http://sites.rootsweb.com/~nsgrdpre/documents/dossiers/Ronnie-Gilles/Acadians-Halifax-Georges-Island-1755-1764-(English).pdf
7. Story of the Acadians, Comeau / Earl J. Comeau: https://www.acadian.org/history/story-acadians-comeau/
8. Pembroke Passenger List Reconstructed / Paul Delaney: http://www.acadian-home.org/Pembroke-list0003.PDF
9. Comeau Family Histories / Jacques A.Comeau: https://comeauhistory.wordpress.com/2016/03/28/a-family-name-some-ancestors-the-comeau-across-france/
10. Early Settlement in Nova Scotia / L.J. Deveau: https://hmhps.ca/pdf/Early-Settlement-in-Nova-Scotia-LJDeveau-March-2018.pdf
11. The Acadians of Louisiana: A Synthesis / Steven A Cormier: http://www.acadiansingray.com/Acadians%20of%20LA-Synthesis-Intro.html#THE_ACADIANS_OF_LOUISIANA
12. The Acadian Response to the Growth of British Power in Nova Scotia, 1749-1755 / W. Peter Ward: https://dalspace.library.dal.ca/bitstream/handle/10222/59441/dalrev_vol51_iss2_pp165_177.pdf?sequence=1&isAllowed=y
13. The Acadian Exiles in England 1756 – 1763 / Dorothy Vinter: https://dalspace.library.dal.ca/bitstream/handle/10222/58722/dalrev_vol36_iss4_pp344_353.pdf?sequence=1

14. Villages des Comeau Chipoudie et La Baie de Chignectou / Paul Surette: http://www.geocities.ws/comeau_famille/chignectou.html
15. L'histoire d'Yamachiche, - Hommage a now familles Acadiennes - Numero 10 -2013 / Andre Desaulniers: http://yamachiche.ca/histoire/histoire-yamachiche-acadiens2013.pdf
16. Colby Cosh: When Acadians and Mik'maq coexisted in a state of peaceful anarchy https://nationalpost.com/opinion/colby-cosh-when-acadians-and-mikmaq-coexisted-in-a-state-of-peaceful-anarchy
17. Minnesota Historical Society: https://www.mnhs.org/people/statecensus
18. Little Falls, MN – Historic Contexts: https://sites.rootsweb.com/~mnmorris/#churches
19. Lumber & labour in the Great Lake: http://collections.mnhs.org/MNHistoryMagazine/articles/36/v36i05p153-16.pdf
20. Canadian Museum of Immigration at Pier 21 - Settling the West: Immigration to the Prairies from 1867 to 1914 / Eric Gagnon https://pier21.ca/research/immigration-history/settling-the-west-immigration-to-the-prairies-from-1867-to-1914
21. The Encyclopedia of Saskatchewan - Association Culturelle Franco-Canadienne: / Andre Lalonde: https://esask.uregina.ca/entry/association_culturelle_franco-canadienne.jsp
22. Chez les Francais du Canada: Les Emigrants, Quebec, Montreal, Ottawa, le grand Ouest, Vancouver / Jean Lionnet: https://gallica.bnf.fr/ark:/12148/bpt6k5773127j/f243.item.texteImage.zoom
23. La Liberte et le Patriote. Winnipeg: 1910-1941: http://peel.library.ualberta.ca/newspapers/LLP
24. La Liberte. Winnipeg: 1913-1941: http://peel.library.ualberta.ca/newspapers/LLT
25. Quebec Parishes Registers BAnQ: https://www.nosorigines.qc.ca/genealogie-paroisses-Quebec.aspx?lng=en
26. Nova Scotia Parish Registers: https://heritage.canadiana.ca/view/oocihm.lac_mikan_101305

27. Nova Scotia Archives::
    https://archives.novascotia.ca/acadian/results/?Search=comeau&fieldSelect=name
28. Port Lajoie PEI records:
    http://anom.archivesnationales.culture.gouv.fr/caomec2/osd.php?territoire=CANADA&commune=ILE%20SAINT-JEAN%20(PORT-LA-JOYE)&annee=1756
29. Acadian Census Records:
    https://heritage.canadiana.ca/view/oocihm.lac_reel_c2572/2
30. Canadian Census: https://www.bac-lac.gc.ca/eng/census/Pages/census.aspx
31. Annapolis Royal – 1733 (notes by Placid Gaudet):
    https://recherche-collection-search.bac-lac.gc.ca/eng/home/record?app=fonandcol&IdNumber=4125285
32. Mapping the deportations - 1755:
    https://www.canadiangeographic.ca/article/mapping-acadian-deportations
33. Chipoudie – 1755 (Comeau Meadows & Young Comeau Village): https://fafa-acadie.org/nouvelles/2-general/131-emplacement-des-familles-acadiennes
34. Sentier Acadie Historique:
    https://sentieracadie.ca/fr/ancetres-acadiens/villages-acadiens
35. Turn of the Century: Minnesota's Population in 1900 and today:
    https://www.lrl.mn.gov/docs/pre2003/other/990581.pdf
36. Chronology of the Deportations & Migrations of theAcadians 1755-1816: http://www.acadian-home.org/Paul-Delaney-Chronology.html
37. Acadian & French Canadian Ancestral Home:
    http://www.acadian-home.org/frames.html
38. Records of the Deportation and Le Grand Dérangement, 1714-1768
    https://archives.novascotia.ca/deportation/archives/?Number=NSHSIII&Page=71

Additional Reading / Stories of Interest:

1. Jacques Rousse: (married to Marie Anne Comeau, daughter of Francois Comeau & Anne Lord)
   https://www.wikitree.com/wiki/Rousse-95
   https://en.wikipedia.org/wiki/Rouses_Point,_New_York
   https://www.geni.com/people/Jacques-Rouse/6000000004077977205
2. Anne Raymond (daughter of Anne Comeau & Francois Raymond):
   https://robertberubeblog.wordpress.com/2017/08/25/1755-anne-raymond-une-acadienne-deportee-sur-le-pembroke-1755-anne-raymond-an-acadienne-deported-on-the-pembroke/
   http://www.acadian-home.org/PD-Pembroke.html
   https://museeacadien.ca/en/the-seizure-of-the-pembrook-by-the-acadians/
3. Francois Raymond (son of Anne Comeau & Francois Raymond):
   https://museeacadien.ca/en/condamnes-a-etre-fouette-avec-le-chat-a-neuf-queues/
4. Antoine Comeau / Anthony Coombs (son of Pierre Comeau & Rose Bayon):
   https://archive.org/details/anthonycoombs2019cw/mode/2up
   https://www.deseret.com/2018/8/26/20652022/reader-voices-finding-a-rich-history-in-novia-scotia-and-maine#on-islesboro-ferry-are-two-coombs-cousins-who-went-on-the-trip-to-find-out-more-about-anthony-coombs-wendy-brimhall-and-dr-douglas-coombs
5. Comeau Family History:
   https://comeauhistory.wordpress.com/2016/03/28/a-family-name-some-ancestors-the-comeau-across-france/
6. Joseph Broussard:
   https://www.albertcountymuseum.com/pirate-of-the-petitcodiac
7. Helenes Des Portes:
   http://www.biographi.ca/en/bio/desportes_helene_1E.html

8. Saskatoon Star Phoenix / Sask Province pays Tribute to 100 year old farms (Omer Como, son of Elzear Comeau & Celina Doucet):
   https://www.pressreader.com/canada/saskatoon-starphoenix/20070613/281552286439153
9. Jacques Vigneau:
   http://cfml.ci.umoncton.ca/1755-html/index830c.html?id=010711000&lang=en&style=G&admin=false&linking=
   http://www.danielnpaul.com/Col/1998/TheRestOfJacquesMaurice%27sStory.html

[1] "Expulsion Orders by Governor Charles Lawrence." Government of Prince Edward Island https://www.princeedwardisland.ca/sites/default/files/publications/eelc_evangeline_appendix_b_8.pdf Accessed 12 October 2021

[2] "Halifax, August 9." The Maryland Gazette, [Numb. 540]. Containing the Freshest Advices foreign and domestic. Thursday, September 11, 1755 https://msa.maryland.gov/megafile/msa/speccol/sc4800/sc4872/001279/html/m1279-0778.html Accessed: 12 March 2023

[3] "Halifax, August 9." The Maryland Gazette, [Numb. 540]. Containing the Freshest Advices foreign and domestic. Thursday, September 11, 1755 https://msa.maryland.gov/megafile/msa/speccol/sc4800/sc4872/001279/html/m1279-0778.html Accessed: 12 March 2023

[4] "Gentlemen." Nova Scotia Archives. Winslow's Journal, part ii, p. 94, p. 95. https://archives.novascotia.ca/deportation/archives/?Number=NSHSIII&Page=94 Accessed 13 March 2023

[5] "Sainte-Gertrude". Fichiers: 1870 Janvier – December. BAnQ Biblioteche et Archives Bibliothèque et Archives nationales du Québec https://numerique.banq.qc.ca/patrimoine/details/52327/4427652?docref=CStuuUYzpK18rI_sj0KLkw Accessed 15 August 2022

[6] Longfellow, Henry Wadsworth. "Evangelina; a tale of Acadie, Cambridge, Printed at the Riverside Press, 1893. Image https://www.loc.gov/item/12036271/ Accessed 29 September 2022

[7] "Died." Little Falls herald. [volume], May 12, 1899, Image 5. Library of Congress https://chroniclingamerica.loc.gov/lccn/sn89064515/1899-05-12/ed-1/seq-5/ Accessed 21 Sep 2021

[8] "$1000 Offered for its Equal." Little Falls Herald weekly transcript., June 26, 1900, SPECIAL TUESDAY EDITION, Image 1. Library of Congress, https://chroniclingamerica.loc.gov/lccn/sn89064526/1900-06-26/ed-1/seq-1/ Accessed 01 March 2023.

[9] "Another Victim of Faith Cure." Little Falls Herald weekly transcript. (Little Falls, Morrison Co., Minn.), 16 Nov. 1900. Chronicling America: Historic American Newspapers. Lib. of Congress. https://chroniclingamerica.loc.gov/lccn/sn89064526/1900-11-16/ed-1/seq-2/ Accessed 09 March 2023

[10] "Two Christian Science Healer." Little Falls weekly transcript. (Little Falls, Morrison Co., Minn.), 31 Oct. 1899. Chronicling America: Historic American Newspapers. Lib. of Congress. https://chroniclingamerica.loc.gov/lccn/sn89064526/1899-10-31/ed-1/seq-7/ Accessed 09 March 2023

[11] "A Touch of Jim Jams." Little Falls Herald weekly transcript., [Volume], October 24, 1899, SPECIAL TUESDAY EDITION, Image 4. Library of Congress. https://chroniclingamerica.loc.gov/lccn/sn89064526/1899-10-24/ed-1/seq-4/ Accessed 16 December 2019

[12] "River Gets One Victim." Little Falls Herald weekly transcript., [Volume], December 15, 1899, REGULAR FRIDAY EDITION, Image 2. Library of Congress. https://chroniclingamerica.loc.gov/lccn/sn89064526/1899-12-15/ed-1/seq-2/ Accessed 18 December 2019

[13] "Shall the City be Wet or Dry? Petition Circulated to Submit Question to Voters at Spring Election." Little Falls herald. [volume], February 19, 1915, Image 1. Library of Congress. https://chroniclingamerica.loc.gov/lccn/sn89064515/1915-02-19/ed-1/seq-1/ Accessed 8 February 2021

[14] "DIED." Little Falls herald. [volume], March 02, 1917, Image 1. Library of Congress. https://chroniclingamerica.loc.gov/lccn/sn89064515/1917-03-02/ed-1/seq-1/ Accessed 15 December 2019

[15] "Food Administration Requires Report on Flour Supplies Be Made By May 1." Little Falls herald. [volume], April 26, 1918, Image 3. Library of Congress. https://chroniclingamerica.loc.gov/lccn/sn89064515/1918-04-26/ed-1/seq-3/

[16] "Report for July. Was Busy time for Home Demonstrator – Bread Contest today." Little Falls herald. [volume], August 8, 1918, Image 1. Library of Congress. https://chroniclingamerica.loc.gov/lccn/sn89064515/1918-08-09/ed-1/seq-1/ Accessed 29 June 2020

[17] "Annual Report of the Department of the Interior for the Year 1893." Part III Immigration, page 146 https://books.google.ca/books?id=mhlOAAAAYAAJ&pg=RA5-PR7&lpg=RA5-PR7&dq Accessed 18 August 2021

[18] "Annual Report of the Department of the Interior for the Year 1893." Part III Immigration, page 146 https://books.google.ca/books?id=mhlOAAAAYAAJ&pg=RA5-PR7&lpg=RA5- Accessed 18 August 2021

[19] "Annual Report of the Department of the Interior for the Year 1893." Part III Immigration, page 155 https://books.google.ca/books?id=mhlOAAAAYAAJ&pg=RA5-PR7&lpg=RA5- Accessed 18 August 2021

[20] Peel 1985: Canada Department of the interior :The great Canadian North-West: Finest farming lands in the world: Homestead of one hundred and sixty acres free: What delegates from various states have to say about it. [Ottawa: Department of the Interior], 1892. D.J. Waggoner, Colonization Agent, Jefferonville, Vermont.
http://peel.library.ualberta.ca/bibliography/1985/1.html Accessed 06 August 2021

[21] Peel 1389: Canadian Pacific Railway. Plain Facts from Farmers in the Canadian North West. London & Manchester, England: H. Blacklock & Co. [1885]
http://peel.library.ualberta.ca/bibliography/1389/1.html Accessed 06 August 2021

[22] "Annual Report of the Department of the Interior for the Year 1893." Part II Dominion Land Surveys, page 50
https://books.google.ca/books?id=rI8_AQAAMAAJ&pg=RA1-
Accessed 18 August 2021

[23] "The Saskatchewan Valley and Manitoba Land Co. Ltd." Ann Arbor Angus Democrat, October 9, 1903.
https://aadl.org/aa_argus_democrat_19031009
Accessed 24 August 2021

[24] "Married." Little Falls herald. [volume], March 5, 1920, Image 1. Library of Congress.
https://chroniclingamerica.loc.gov/lccn/sn89064515/1920-03-05/ed-1/seq-1/ Accessed 17 December 2019

www.ingramcontent.com/pod-product-compliance
Lightning Source LLC
Chambersburg PA
CBHW031105080526
44587CB00011B/831